CONNECTING LINES

OTHER BOOKS

by Robert Leichtman, M.D. & Carl Japikse

Active Meditation: The Western Tradition
Forces of the Zodiac
The Art of Living (five volumes)
The Life of Spirit (five volumes)
Healing Lines
Ruling Lines

by Robert Leichtman, M.D.

From Heaven to Earth (6 books)

by Carl Japikse

The Light Within Us
Exploring the Tarot
The Hour Glass
The Tao of Meow
The Biggest Tax Cheat in America is the I.R.S.

CONNECTING LINES

A New Interpretation
of the I Ching
For Understanding
Personal Relationships

By Robert R. Leichtman, M.D.
and Carl Japikse

ARIEL PRESS
Atlanta, Georgia

No royalties are paid on this book

This book is made possible
by a gift to the Publications Fund of Light
by Judy Ross

CONNECTING LINES

ISBN 0-89804-092-2

The I Ching

The I Ching is one of the best systems of "practical philosophy" ever devised. Philosophy is meant to be the pursuit of truth and wisdom. The word itself means "the love of knowledge." But modern philosophy has lost track of its roots. Too often, the pursuit of truth has been replaced by a debate of ideas. Debates can be fascinating, of course, but they tend to polarize thinking, not unite it. As a result, modern philosophy has become fragmented and disconnected, leading to such aberrations of thought as existentialism.

Worst of all, the study of philosophy has become so specialized that it no longer speaks to the average person, even the well-educated average person. It has become impractical. The great ideas of philosophy no longer shape daily thinking and behavior as they once did. Philosophy has become abstruse and esoteric, the plaything of theorists living in the proverbial ivory tower.

This is not what philosophy is meant to be. It is meant to be a practical source of values, mental principles, and guidance upon which intelligent people can base their thinking. It should be accessible at least to the educated, if not to every man and woman in the market place. Ideally, it should be a body of ideas that can be easily consulted and relied upon for a determination of basic values, self-examination, and all types of decision making.

It is interesting that the I Ching has been gaining popularity in the West at the same time that our own philosophical systems are becoming more and more arcane. The average intelligent person senses a need for a practical philosophical system, even if the academics and intellectuals do not. And so an increasing number of people are turning to the I Ching, and discovering that it embodies a great deal of truth and insight that can be easily tapped.

The I Ching is a "practical" system because it can be consulted for practical insight and solutions into the ordinary problems of daily living—business decisions, health problems, the challenge of raising children, and so on. Those who do not understand the I Ching sometimes think of it as a system of fortune telling, but it is not. It is a philosophical system that has been developed by some of the greatest minds China has produced. The fact that it can be used by people of average intelligence to help make sense of their lives, as well as the highly educated, only serves to broaden its value, not diminish it.

The Chinese have worked with the I Ching for thousands of years. In the West, we have worked with it for about fifty years, and only intensely for half of that time. It was Carl Jung's work with the I Ching, more than anything else, that brought this remarkable system to the attention of a large number of people.

Because of the relatively short time we have worked with this system, most people still find it somewhat puzzling to use at times. This is because the commentaries on the I Ching have all been translations of the original Chinese texts, written by

Chinese philosophers using the Chinese language and Chinese thought patterns to communicate with Chinese. This is perfectly normal. But a Westerner wanting insight into how to deal with a cranky neighbor may find it a little daunting to try to understand what the I Ching is answering, if using one of the standard texts.

Recognizing this problem, we decided it was time to do something to correct it. In specific, we saw the enormous potential of using the modern computer to help make the ancient guidance of the I Ching even more practical for the Western mind.

The object was not just to program the computer to construct the hexagrams by random process; after all, this is something that can be done just as easily with three coins! The purpose of computerizing the I Ching was to create a series of modules that could be rapidly accessed by the computer, depending upon the kind of question the user wished to ask. In this way, the commentary of each hexagram could be specifically tailored to the kind of inquiry being made.

In other words, if the user wished to ask a question about health, he or she would direct the computer to select the health module. If the question pertained to relationships, the user would select that module on the computer's menu. The question would then be typed in, the hexagram generated by random selection, and the appropriate commentary would appear.

All that remained to be done was develop a computer program—and to write the text for several different modules!

The computer program, *I Ching On Line*, was developed by James D. Davis, Ph.D., a retired professor of mathematics from Fairleigh Dickinson University. His program for the IBM PC and compatibles first appeared in 1989 and was greeted with high critical acclaim. Dr. Davis was in the process of developing a companion program for the Macintosh when he died.

James Watson, a computer expert at NC Assistant, stepped in, developing a program that takes advantage of the Macintosh's unique capabilities.

This book is the text of the third module developed. It deals exclusively with understanding human relationships.

The first module, dealing with health questions, was issued in 1989. The book containing the text of that module is called *Healing Lines*. The second module is designed to support the decision making process, both in business and personal life. The book containing the text is called *Ruling Lines*.

In writing the text for each of these books, we have avoided making a direct translation. Instead, we intuitively "dissected" each hexagram and examined it in its original, archetypal form, then restated these basic ideas so that they apply directly to questions about interpersonal relationships, in terms that can be understood by modern Westerners.

One more module remains to be written. The book will be called *Changing Lines*, and the text will be focused on helping us accelerate and understand our personal and spiritual growth. Throughout all four modules, our goal is to help make the I Ching the tool of practical philosophy it was designed to be. We make no apologies for clarity and the specific focus we have given the text. We are fully aware that many specialists in the I Ching feel that its great strength is its vagueness, which forces the user to utilize his or her intuition. But truth and wisdom are never vague or confusing. They are always simple, clear, and insightful. It is usually a sign of intellectual laziness to fail to make the attempt to communicate this simplicity, clarity, and vision to others in easily understood terms.

Ideally, the text that follows is meant to be used as an adjunct to *I Ching On Line*. Nevertheless, we also know that many people do not own a personal computer, or perhaps do not have a model which will run the program. These people can still use the text for relationships—and the others in the set—by using the commentary in this book to interpret the hexagrams they generate by more traditional methods.

Our work is done. Now yours begins. The I Ching can become a source of practical philosophy for you only if you use it for that purpose. If you ask the I Ching silly, irreverent questions, it will give you flippant answers. If you try to use it as a crutch or a scapegoat, it will in essence tell you to stop using it until you are more honest in your pursuit of knowledge. But if you use it sincerely, to try to make sense out of the difficult, confusing issues of life, you will discover a source of unlimited guidance and insight.

The I Ching is meant to be used. Use it wisely, and you will see the results in more intelligent decisions!

How The I Ching Works

The I Ching is a system of archetypal forces, based on the principles of duality and the constancy of change. In China, the component forces of this duality are *yin* and *yang*. In English, we might call them positive and negative, male and female, or point and counterpoint.

The philosophers of ancient China observed that duality and change do not occur capriciously. The phenomena of life arise from a dynamic interaction of dualities. For this reason, there cannot be growth without resistance—or opportunity without hardship, success without failure.

To put this principle in terms of change, as one situation improves, another will decline. As one issue evolves, a second will decay. As the life of one movement grows in vitality, a competitive movement will lose momentum. As the level of competence in one group rises, it sinks in another.

The principle of duality governs all movements in life. And as these dual forces interact with one another, they generate complex change.

Since the Chinese language is based on pictographs, rather than letters, it was natural for the philosophers to translate this idea into images. But these are very abstract images, as befits the basic concept of duality. The symbol for active force was a single straight line; the symbol for passive force was a broken line.

THE EIGHT TRIGRAMS

Heaven

Lake

Fire

Thunder

Wind

Water

Mountain

Earth

The first combination of these solid and broken lines was to form a set of eight trigrams, each containing three lines. These eight trigrams are illustrated on the previous page. To these trigrams, philosophers began attaching meanings and interpretations, just as the ancient astrologers ascribed meanings to the constellations in the sky. And so, the trigram Heaven took on the meaning of raw creative energy and universal purpose. The trigram Fire, by contrast, took on the meaning of awareness—the fiery mind and brilliance.

Eventually, these trigrams were put together, one on top of the other, to form hexagrams. The upper trigram came to represent the larger picture of any situation—the view from heaven, as it were. The lower trigram came to represent the individualized focus of our daily problems.

There are a total of sixty-four hexagrams, but sixty-four is not the important number. Two is. Each hexagram is the direct result of duality and change, because each hexagram is composed of six lines, each of which is either solid or broken. Positive or negative. Active or passive.

As the system evolved, the ancient Chinese philosophers realized that few situations in life remain stagnant for very long. The hexagrams are not just abstract images—they are symbols for dynamic, active forces. And so every hexagram has the potential to change into any one of the other sixty-three, or remain static.

The first hexagram represents the basic definition of a situation, as it exists now.

The second indicates what the inherent energies of the situation are leading to.

It is this capacity to represent moving, living forces that makes the I Ching ("I Ching" means "Book of Change") such a valuable tool of practical philosophy. Each hexagram is linked with a specific archetypal force affecting human life. As we use the I Ching to understand our problems and challenges, we begin to perceive what dynamic forces are active in our life, and where they are leading us. Patterns emerge, leading to insight.

Using the I Ching is very simple. If you have a computer and *I Ching On Line,* just call up the program, type in your question, and follow the directions to generate the hexagrams. [For more detailed help, refer to the instructions which come with the program.]

If you do not have a computer, you can generate the hexagrams by using three coins. Having thought of your question (it is best to write it down), you construct the hexagrams by tossing the coins six times. Each time you toss the three coins, there are four possible ways they can land:

• All three coins can be heads. This represents a broken line, changing. [▬▬ ▬▬ •]

• All three coins can be tails. This represents a solid line, changing. [▬▬▬▬▬ •]

• Two coins can be heads and one a tail. This represents an unchanging solid line. [▬▬▬▬▬]

• Two coins can be tails and one a head. This represents an unchanging broken line. [▬▬ ▬▬]

The Chinese work from the bottom up. Therefore, the first toss generates the bottom line of the hexagram. The second toss generates the line above it, and so on, until all six lines are determined, from bottom to top.

It is helpful to develop some kind of annotation indicating changing lines. This can be a dot (●) to the right of the line or, as we use in the computer program, a triangle (▲). The changing lines enable you to construct the second hexagram, or resolution. All unchanging lines in the first hexagram remain the same in the second hexagram. But a solid line that is changing in the first hexagram becomes a broken line in the second, and a broken line that is changing becomes a solid line. These changing lines indicate the principle of duality in action, moving from pole to pole.

In other words, hexagram #28, The Onslaught, is composed of a broken, four solid, and a broken line, reading from the bottom up. If lines 2 and 3 are changing, then they create a completely different hexagram, #45, Partnership, which is composed of three broken, two solid, and a broken line, from the bottom up.

The first hexagram defines the issue at hand. Each changing line reveals the subtle energies influencing conditions. The second hexagram indicates how the situation will be resolved.

If there are no changing lines in the first hexagram, then the situation is considered static. A second hexagram is not constructed.

In advanced uses of the I Ching, a third hexagram is generated as well. This is called the *nuclear* hexagram. It is derived by taking the second, third, and fourth lines (from the bottom up) of the first hexagram and transliterating them as the first, second, and third lines of the nuclear hexagram. The third, fourth, and fifth lines of the original hexagram are then transliterated as the fourth, fifth, and sixth lines of the nuclear.

There are only sixteen hexagrams which serve as nuclear hexagrams, each one being produced by four different hexagrams. These are obviously the most potent hexagrams of the sixty-four, representing primary archetypal forces. In general, the nuclear hexagram indicates the ideal methodology to use in handling the situation at hand.

Once these three hexagrams are generated, the process of interpretation can begin. If aided by *I Ching On Line,* the appropriate commentary will flash on the screen with just a touch of a key or the click of a mouse. But even without a computer, the process of interpretation is still relatively easy.

Determine the number of each of the three hexagrams. Then, starting with the first hexagram, turn to the appropriate page in this book and read the commentary on the left hand page. This commentary is broken into three sections. The first is a general, overall statement about the forces affecting the subject of your inquiry. The second comments on relationships in which the other party is dominant. The third section comments on relationships in which the other party is subordinate to you.

Read these comments carefully and reflect on them. It is often wise to reread the text several times, to make sure you fully understand it.

Next, read whatever text on the right hand page corresponds to the changing lines that apply to your consultation. In other words, if lines 2 and 3 are changing, read only the text for lines 2 and 3. Discount the rest. Should there be no changing lines, read only the text entitled "Unchanging."

Once you have digested the commentary for the first hexagram and its changing lines, turn to the pages which comment on the second hexagram, the Resolution. Read the text on the left-hand page, but do not read any of the changing lines.

Finally, consult the text for the nuclear hexagram, again reading just the text on the left-hand page.

If you are serious about understanding more about yourself and life in general, it would be a good idea to keep a record of your I Ching consultations. Write down your question, list the hexagrams that are generated, and then make notes about the insights and conclusions you derive from reading the text. Date each entry, so you can refer back to it easily at a later time.

Of course, if you are using *I Ching On Line,* the computer does all this record keeping for you.

Formulating Questions

Because of the unique module feature of *I Ching On Line,* it is usually relatively easy to interpret the answers you get while using the text of *Connecting Lines.* The text is written on the assumption that the user is asking a question pertaining to a human relationship. It is not the intent of the I Ching to dictate to the user exactly what he or she should or should not do, however. The purpose of the I Ching is to reveal the larger context in which the situation at hand is unfolding, so that the decision made will be the most intelligent one possible. As long as the question fits these parameters, the answers provided by the text in *Connecting Lines* should be relatively straightforward.

This is not to say that this text cannot be used for questions that do not strictly fit this pattern. Like any good system of divination, this text can be used to answer any legitimate question. But the farther afield the question wanders from the focus of the module—understanding relationships—the more intuitive the interpretation will have to be to arrive at the truth.

In writing the text for *Connecting Lines,* we have tried to help you in this stage of formulating intelligent questions. Knowing that few relationships are actually based on true equality—equal duties, equal initiative, equal talent, and equal recognition—we have divided our comments into two groups: dominant and subordinate.

Read the **dominant** commentary if you believe

this is a relationship in which the other person (or people) are dominant in regards to you.

Read the **subordinate** commentary if you believe this is a relationship in which the other person (or people) are subordinate in regards to you.

A parent inquiring about a child, for example, would read the subordinate commentary, because the child is subordinate to him or her.

An employee inquiring about his relationship with his boss would read the dominant commentary, because the boss is dominant.

In many instances, it will be instantly clear what kind of relationship you have. In others, it may take a great deal of reflection to decide. In fact, the issue of dominance-subordinance may often switch back and forth as you ask different questions about the same relationship.

In a marriage, for instance, the husband will be dominant in some areas, the wife in others. An aged parent, who has insisted on dominance for years and years, may become subordinant when too old to care for himself or herself.

Indeed, the issue of dominance and subordinance can become extremely subtle. Some people are actually so skillful in managing their weaknesses and dependency that they become dominant, even though they appear to be subordinate.

In these kinds of cases, therefore, it is best to read both commentaries, with the idea of letting them help you decide the best tone for you to set: should you be dominant or subordinate in dealing with this person?

For this—and other good reasons—be sure to take

whatever amount of time is necessary to formulate an intelligent, penetrating question. Do not rush through this preliminary stage. Think carefully. Reflect on your situation. What do you need to know?

Some people do not use questions. They assume that the I Ching knows better than they do what they need to hear, so they simply toss the coins without troubling themselves with a question.

This is not desirable. The I Ching does know what you need to hear, but it is incapable of communicating it to you unless you create a strong invocation for the answer. This invocation is created by focusing a potent need to know. The more intelligently and precisely you formulate your question, the better the results will be.

In using *Connecting Lines,* it is also good to keep in mind that there is a difference between snooping and asking for intelligent guidance. If you try to ask a question such as, "Is John cheating on me?" the I Ching is likely to answer, in so many words, "Mind your own business." In point of fact, it will probably give you a stern lecture about the need to build a relationship on a solid foundation of trust and respect, not weaken it with suspicion and gossipy speculation.

The best kind of questions are those that will lead you toward a deeper understanding of this bond:

How can I improve my relationship with Will?

What are the inner dimensions of my tie with Julie?

How well would Melissa fit into our work unit?

Why do I get headaches whenever I spend a lot of time with Sammy?

19

What is the best way to deal with Martha's angry outbursts?

How can I best help Diana improve her performance at school?

What changes must I make now that my husband is retired and spending more time at home?

What tone should I set in the upcoming interview with Mr. Tucker?

What must I do to mend fences with Mary?

What is the best way to deal with John?

What motivated my parents to criticize me so much while I was growing up?

How can I muster the strength to forgive Nat?

Just about any question pertaining to a relationship is fine, so long as it does not require a "yes" or "no" answer. The I Ching is not especially suited to yes or no questions; its purpose is to provide insight and understanding.

You can even ask nonpersonal questions. The principles of interpersonal relationships apply to groups as well as individuals, so you can ask questions such as:

What should be the company's attitude toward its competitors?

What changes are needed to produce a lasting peace in the Middle East?

What is the best way to help the homeless?

It is important, however, to show respect for the I Ching. For this reason, do not ask the same question repeatedly, either because you did not understand the original answer or (the more common motivation) because you did not like the answer. If you are confused by an answer, it is perfectly all right to ask for a clarification—just do not ask the exact same question again.

As an example, assume you have asked: "How can I improve my relationship with my children?" One of the changing lines informs you: "You will need as much goodwill and forgiveness as you can muster to actually turn this relationship around, but it can be done." If you are unsure just what you must forgive, ask a second question: "What obstacle have I created by being unwilling to forgive in interacting with my children?"

In fact, one question will often lead to a whole series of other questions, just as a tiny pebble thrown into the middle of a pond will produce ripple after ripple of concentric emanations. Keep alert for possible questions and pursue the implications of your query—and its answer—to the furthest extent possible.

The I Ching will never tire of your questions, as long as they are valid and sincere. You are limited only by your own imagination—and your personal need to know.

21

A Word of Caution

The one thing you can be sure of is that the I Ching will answer your question! This is why it is important to formulate it precisely, write it down, and keep a record of it. The I Ching will not answer the question you *meant* to ask, nor the question you *should have* asked. It will answer the question you actually did ask, as you worded it.

The question you ask becomes frozen in time, once you have generated the hexagrams that answer it. You cannot go back after the fact and reword your question—or reinterpret it because a different question will seem to fit your interpretation of the answer better! It may seem unnecessary to make a point as obvious as this, but sometimes it is the most obvious aspects of life that cause us the most trouble. So it is with the I Ching. The most common cause of confusion in using this system is poor memory. People have an enormous capacity for self-deception, and this extends to asking questions of the I Ching. Once they begin reading the commentary, they often unconsciously change the question they asked—even if they have a written record of it! They alter the question in small ways so that the answer is more favorable to them—or at least less threatening.

As an example, let's say you ask the question: "What will be the outcome of my dispute with my neighbor?" The answer might indicate that the dispute itself is a silly overreaction to an imagined insult. The result will therefore be a continued estrangement between the two of you, until you decide your reaction was indeed silly and make amends. Given your present attitude, you might then conclude that there is nothing to do, since it is clear your neighbor is not going to give in. But the question was not, "When will my neighbor admit he was wrong?" It was: "What will be the outcome of my dispute with my neighbor?" And the answer, quite correctly, indicated that the current schism will continue until you have a change of heart. To understand the answer, therefore, you need to stick to the original question—not make up a new one that fits your need for self-deception!

Obviously, it is of great importance to eliminate this kind of self-deception in using the I Ching. Make a written record of your question, and then refer back to it again and again as you read the commentary and formulate your interpretation of it. If you do not understand the question, after all, it will be impossible to understand the answer!

In using the I Ching, the keynote should always be self-examination. We are looking for new insight into the inner workings of the events and problems of our life—not for new excuses, or new scapegoats, or new rationalizations. If you are prone to self-deception, the first question you need to ask the I Ching is: "How can I best protect myself from my self-deception?" Only when this question is fully answered, and acted upon, should you then proceed with others.

Divine Intelligence

In using the I Ching, the big question to the Westerner is always: "How does this thing work?" We have elevated skepticism to such a high level that almost everyone asks this question when first exposed to the I Ching. Curiously, it is not a common question in China. As a culture, the Chinese are not puzzled by how the I Ching works. The only thing that puzzles them is why the average Westerner makes such a big fuss about it!

They have a point. The Judeo-Christian tradition is the major moral and philosophical basis for thinking in the West; it is common for Westerners to profess a belief in the omnipresence, omnipotence, and omniscience of God. "Omniscience" means not only that God is all-knowing, but on a more practical level, that divine intelligence pervades everything. Whether we are at worship, in our car, at home, or at the grocery, we are surrounded and interpenetrated by divine intelligence (and love and power!) at all times.

Isn't it odd, therefore, that there are so many people who will stand up in church or temple and proclaim divine omniscience, then act as though they left it all behind the moment they stepped outside! But they do—they believe in luck, in random sequences, and in accidents, not in divine omniscience. Frankly, it's not a record that any of us should be proud of.

Divine intelligence is designed to give us the answers we seek. If we are sufficiently enlightened we should be able to discern these answers from any common phenomenon of life—as Brother Lawrence did centuries ago as he watched the leaves fall from trees in autumn and came to understand God's benevolent love and protection.

Since most of us are not this enlightened, special systems have been developed over the eons to help us communicate more easily with divine intelligence. The I Ching is one of these systems. It works because divine intelligence pervades all of life and every event of life, even something as trivial as the "random" throw of three coins or the way in which you strike your computer keyboard six times in succession.

The random action of throwing the coins or striking computer keys is not what triggers the right response; it merely helps us get our own wish life and preconceived ideas out of the way, so that we do not control the process. Once we are unable to consciously influence the selection process of the hexagrams, then divine intelligence is able to take over. Time after time, the right hexagrams are generated to answer our questions.

It is for this reason that we need to take the answers the I Ching provides seriously. And we must also always keep in mind the full context of our questions and answers.

In a very real sense, our personal world is a small but complete universe which exists as a part of the larger universe of our family, our work, our community, our nation, and humanity as a whole. As we develop personal problems, we can only understand them if we are able to see them in the larger context of these bigger spheres of influence. This is true whether the problem involves health, business, relationships, or just our own ethics and inner stability.

The I Ching is designed to help us see our connections to these larger spheres. We may believe that our problem exists only within the microcosm of our private world, but in truth the solution, whatever it is, always lies in the macrocosm. Unless we can reach out to the macrocosm and discover what the solution is, it will evade us.

Divine intelligence is not just a huge cosmic brain. It is a force field of intelligence, filled with living, dynamic energies. These energies are what are known as "archetypal forces." They are the abstract forces from which everything that is has emerged.

Love, wisdom, and power are the three most basic of these forces. Others include grace, joy, beauty, peace, harmony, and abundance. Whenever we have a problem, it is a sign that we lack one of these archetypal forces, or are misusing it. We will not be able to find it within our own private world, however. We must reach out to the macrocosm for it.

The I Ching is one of the great tools for guiding us to the right force and helping us connect with it. In fact, the inner structure of the I Ching makes it clear that this system was designed with just this purpose in mind. The lower trigram in each hexagram represents the microcosm—our private world and needs. The higher trigram represents the inner dimensions of life, the view from heaven. It does not reveal our personal world, but the larger macrocosm in which we live and move and have our being.

Given this basic structure, there are many subtle clues that can help us comprehend the I Ching more completely. It is often useful, for example, to examine each trigram in a hexagram and go back to its original meanings. Hexagram #28, for example, is composed of the trigram for joy in the upper position and the trigram for gentle influences in the lower one. By seeing the component parts in this way, it is easier to understand why this particular hexagram is called "The Onslaught." The tremendous power above may overwhelm the modest capacity for self-expression below, but if we are able to stretch our skills and talents beyond their normal ability, we can likewise seize an unparalleled opportunity. It is the archetypal energies themselves that create the danger, as they intersect—but it is up to us to determine if these forces will produce a breakthrough, or a breakdown.

This illustrates a point that needs emphasis. Being symbols of archetypal forces, no hexagram is either good or bad. They are all divine. It is up to us to determine how they will be used. If we use these forces wisely, they will be productive. If we use them selfishly, they will be restrictive. The choice is up to us. Our future lies not in the hexagrams themselves, but in our capacity to harness their potential intelligently.

Some of the titles we have chosen for the hexagrams may at times sound ominous: The Wrong Foot, Ruin, Intimidation, Damage Control, and Shakeup.

Others may appeal to us much more: Blossoming, Breakthrough, and Fellowship. But these are just labels for forces which are neither positive nor negative. They are building blocks to be used creatively. A wise person will recognize as much potential for advancement in a time of Disappointment as in a time of Mutual Creativity, and will act accordingly.

Another key to interpreting the hexagrams is what is known as "ruling lines." A ruling line is something like the accented syllable or syllables in a word: it is the line (or sometimes two lines) that dominates all the other lines in the hexagram. In most texts, the ruling lines are indicated as part of the commentary. We have not done so in the text for *Connecting Lines* or any other module, and for a very simple reason. In many consultations of the I Ching, the ruling line will not even appear. Yet if there are three changing lines, one will be dominant for that question, even if none of the changing lines happens to be the natural ruler. If a ruling line has already been picked, it does not encourage the user to try to determine the dominant line. So we have left out the ruling lines, in the hope that the more ambitious users of this text will develop the intuitive habit of determining the true ruler, question by question.

As you read the changing lines, therefore, try to weigh which one is the strongest influence on your situation. It may be perfectly obvious, or it may be obscure. But often once you determine which line is the true ruling force, it gives you the clue you need to interpret the rest of the message. It lets you embrace the inner forces that are at work in this situation.

Ultimately, this is what the I Ching is meant to be: a barometer of the inner forces which influence us individually and collectively. Treat it with respect, but do not be in awe of it. It is a tool that intelligent people use to understand life. If at any point in your use of the I Ching you are unsure of how to proceed next, do not become flustered. Always remember that you have at your disposal one of the greatest tools of divination ever invented. Just ask the I Ching to show you what to do next—and it will!

A NUMBERED GUIDE

TO THE

SIXTY-FOUR HEXAGRAMS

OF THE I CHING

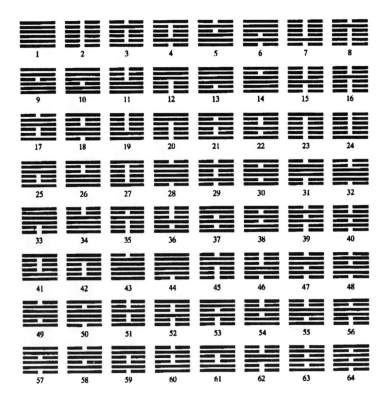

CONNECTING LINES

1. Mutual Creativity

There exists a powerful opportunity for expanding the importance of this relationship in your life. In some way, the time is ripe to seek out and find a fuller measure of the rich inner potential that draws the two of you together. In a marriage, this could be a sign that the time is favorable for starting a family—or to undertake new activities that will draw the two of you more closely together. In a work partnership, it could indicate that new ways of using your skills and talents to complement one another can be developed. Be sure to include everyone who shares your responsibility in the decision making process, however.

Dominant: The best course of action at this time is to cooperate with those in positions of authority or power. The more you can help them attain their goals, the more you share in the power of their trust.

Subordinate: Do not hesitate to act decisively in initiating new plans and policies. At the same time, however, make sure that you communicate your vision of your goals and purposes clearly to those whom you expect to follow your lead.

THE CHANGING LINES

6: Your relationship is not entirely healthy. You support each other's fantasies and self-deceptions more than you make a mutual contribution together.
5: The most important relationship to cultivate at this moment is your tie with the higher self.
4: Heed the dictates of your commitments and duties in setting priorities in this relationship.
3: Do not be swayed by the flattery of sycophants; make sure the people you deal with are sincere and trustworthy—and have something to contribute.
2: You are in a subordinate position. Determine who has the true authority in this situation and cultivate a strong bond with him or her.
1: Lay the groundwork for your mutual creativity, but do not take action yet. Be patient; wait for the right opportunity.

Unchanging: The time is proper to solidify this relationship. Do not be afraid to make suggestions to expand the relationship; as long as you are in tune with your mutual purpose, you can rely on a positive response.

2. Helpfulness

In dealing with others at this time, it is important to listen openly to their ideas and desires and be guided accordingly. Self-centeredness and stubborn resistance to the suggestions of others will lead quickly to disaster. So will the temptation to blame the other person for any problems the relationship might be having. Look at these difficulties as mutual problems to be met and solved together. Try to improve the relationship by determining ways you can respond more openly and helpfully to the mutual needs of the relationship. The keynote of your efforts should be helpfulness.

Dominant: You need to accept the practical limitations of your position gracefully. Let those in power rule, for they bear the responsibility. Your duty is to cooperate with them wisely and helpfully. This is a creative challenge in its own right.

Subordinate: Your own weakness or sensitivity may encourage others to test your power or rebel against you. Their reaction may seem unfair, but you must recognize that you have brought it on yourself.

THE CHANGING LINES

6: Your unyielding perspectives are leading inevitably to a major confrontation. Be more flexible—more open to the purpose of the relationship.
5: There is much you do not understand about this relationship and the role you have played in creating problems. Become a constructive force!
4: Resist the temptation to use the appearance of weakness as a way to manipulate others. Treat others with respect, helpfulness, and integrity.
3: Don't be trapped in self-centeredness. There is a danger of hurting someone just by overlooking his or her needs, in favor of your own. Be helpful!
2: Don't be blinded by hurt feelings. This relationship is too valuable to be jeopardized by self-pity. Be a peacemaker, not a trouble maker.
1: This relationship is coming apart at the seams. Unless you redefine its value to you and restore its vitality, it may be increasingly difficult to sustain it.

Unchanging: This relationship seems to be based more on mutual alienation to society than on any constructive purpose. Unless you can put it on a more positive basis, so that it becomes a helpful factor in life, it will eventually destroy itself.

3. The Wrong Foot

Some relationships start out, as they say, on the wrong foot. Each person makes a bad impression on the other; confusion reigns. This is one of those relationships. Whether immediately obvious or not, there have been misunderstandings and confusion from the very beginning. You are not operating on the same wavelength. This is not to say, however, that this relationship cannot be repaired. To do so, you will have to go back and determine the obstacles that were created in the very early stages of the relationship, and develop a strategy for treating these problems. Then, it will also be necessary to define a new sense of purpose for the relationship, so that it is recast in a positive mold. If you cannot do this for yourself, you may need to seek outside counseling to put this relationship back in perspective.

Dominant: You have expectations about this relationship that simply are not realistic. You are making this person compensate for the problems and errors you have experienced with others in the past. This is not fair.

Subordinate: It is your responsibility to nurture growth in the other person or people involved. Unfortunately, you are probably creating more obstacles to their success than you are being helpful.

THE CHANGING LINES

6: You have chosen to forget the early difficulties you experienced in this situation. This is unwise, for you are now heading in an unfortunate direction.
5: Others are willing to let you take the lead. Do not abuse this opportunity; act wisely.
4: This relationship could well develop into something more than it appears at first. Give it time to flourish.
3: You are being called upon to cast your lot with a person or group you do not know well enough. Carefully review your own values before making any promises or commitments.
2: In the midst of confusion and instability, it is best to rely on your knowledge of who you are. Don't let others tell you who you ought to be.
1: Do not be in a hurry to evaluate new relationships. Relax and enjoy them for what they are, without becoming entangled in them.

Unchanging: The problems you are facing today have characterized this relationship from the very outset. Unless you are willing to face these issues and resolve them, conditions will not improve.

4. Foolishness

You are letting your own immaturity and lack of experience blind you to the true dynamics of this relationship. As a result, you have placed yourself in a position where you can be cheated, conned, or abused and not even recognize it until it is too late. You are being blinded by superficial elements, instead of building a mature relationship based on shared goals and common interests. You need to carefully examine the assumptions and foundation this relationship is built upon, and not be distracted any longer by childish foolishness. If necessary, seek out guidance from someone wiser than yourself.

Dominant: Your tendency to resist being guided, or even to rebel outright, is a liability in this relationship, not an asset. Learn to respect the good and noble elements within the other person, instead of resenting them. Curb any feelings of jealousy, before they do harm.

Subordinate: You can't blame children for acting childishly, but if they are adults, they need to be reminded of their shared responsibility. Do not let subordinates upset your direction by being argumentative or defiant.

THE CHANGING LINES

6: If you feel frustrated or trapped in this relationship, it is only because the habits and traits of the other person mirror similar patterns of your own.

5: Uncritical acceptance of what others claim to be true is apt to get you into a lot of trouble.

4: Submit gracefully to those who are wiser than yourself; be guided by them.

3: Think for yourself; do not get drawn into an immature action just because everyone else is doing it.

2: Do not be quick to judge others, lest you be judging them on the basis of your own selfish motives.

1: Self-restraint should be the byword. Take care not to commit unnecessary gaffes; use a little tact.

Unchanging: You are gaining useful experience through this relationship. Do not dwell on those things that irritate you and make the relationship a difficult one; instead, concentrate on the new insights and understanding you are gaining through this bond.

5. On Hold

No matter how well we plan, there come times in life when activities, changes, and even relationships must be put on hold, to allow for the cyclic order of life to catch up. During a recession, for example, plans to borrow money may have to be put on hold; we must wait for a more propitious time. This is the case in terms of the mutual plans you have been developing in the relationship at hand. Do not rush precipitously into new responsibilities or commitments. Be patient and let these proposals—and your own prospects—develop further before making a final determination.

Dominant: Do not argue or protest when those with more authority than you put the brakes on an idea or project that you are excited about. Use the time of this seeming delay to refine your ideas and build new support for your plans.

Subordinate: This is a time of potential ill will, because not everyone may understand the need for patience and restraint as clearly as you do. If your actions now are too harsh, they may evoke a reaction that will damage morale or even undermine your position.

THE CHANGING LINES

6: The cue to act will arrive soon, if you are able to recognize it.

5: Your most important relationship right now is with your higher self. It is acting, even though physical events may be on hold. If you can grasp the fluid dynamics of the inner life now, it will become easy to wait for the right time physically.

4: Act only with humility and a deep respect for the integrity of others. If you take actions that others perceive as harmful, you may suffer greatly.

3: Do not worry about this relationship. If it is based on shared values, it will survive the threats of the present—and may even become stronger.

2: Your ideas are good, but the timing is wrong. If you act now, people close to you will not understand why, and you will become a target of criticism.

1: Impatient action at this time will introduce new stresses into your relationship. Take it easy!

Unchanging: There are inner dimensions to this relationship you are unaware of. Even now, changes are unfolding at unconscious levels which will alter everything. It is imperative to wait and see what these changes involve before taking action.

41

6. Confrontation

There is too much of a tendency to personalize this relationship and create a battlefield of distress and hurt feelings, rather than engage in mutual expression. You need to learn that it is possible to be supportive of another person without losing your own sense of individuality. It is likewise possible to solve conflicts in a relationship without exacting a *quid pro quo*. Think of this relationship as a shared experience in which you both are striving together to achieve common goals. While conflicts indicate differing values or perspectives, it is important to put the emphasis on what you have in common, not what potentially separates you. In this way, you can learn to solve problems without being confrontational.

Dominant: Now is not a time to stage a big confrontation about disagreements and unresolved issues. Be supportive and conciliatory; it may even be best at times to overlook a deliberate attempt to start a quarrel and reestablish common ground.

Subordinate: Do not put excessive pressure on others; ease off. You may well be alienating others by unwittingly driving wedges between your interests and theirs. If you act thoughtlessly now, you may succeed in drawing out the worst from your friends and colleagues.

THE CHANGING LINES

6: The steps you are contemplating are guaranteed to lead you into confrontations of the worst type. Re-examine your proposals carefully.

5: The conflict you are experiencing in this relationship is symbolic of a deeper confrontation between your personal will and the intent of the higher self. You must resolve this inner issue before the outer problem can be healed.

4: You have painted yourself into a corner. If you fight, you will suffer great loss. Yield gracefully.

3: The root of your conflict lies in clashing values or world views. Try to nurture a healthier respect for the principles of others, instead of believing you must convert everyone to your point of view.

2: Do not add fuel to the fire by trying to defend your pride or your hurt feelings. Try to mend the rift.

1: Do not make this conflict worse, by continuing it. If you have the courage to forgive and get on with life, much good will come.

Unchanging: You are at fundamental odds with the other person involved. Unless you are able to be less rigid, there is little chance for a reconciliation.

7. Peer Pressure

The direction of this relationship is not being guided just by your own individual wishes and decisions; it is being influenced to a large degree by the family, social, and cultural context in which it exists. It has been shaped, in other words, at least in part by what might be called "peer pressure"—the expectations or traditions of your family, your friends, or even such social units as church groups. It is important not to alienate yourselves from these groups, because without their support or approval, your relationship will become distorted. Learn to harmonize your needs with the needs and traditions of these larger groups.

Dominant: Seek out people of authority and stature within the groups to which you belong, and align yourself with their efforts. In this way, you can become a more effective part of the whole.

Subordinate: Tremendous power to achieve your goals can be tapped at this time if you rally the support of those who might wish to help you. Do not demand this support, however; instead, try to inspire it.

THE CHANGING LINES

6: Be sure to express appreciation to those who have helped you achieve your goals.

5: Choose a role model of maturity and wisdom to help you in this situation; do not just go with whatever feels right.

4: You are acting without the blessing of those in power. This makes it almost impossible to achieve your goals.

3: Authority is being ignored, perhaps even ridiculed. Your own activities cannot flourish until this condition is corrected.

2: You are in rapport with others on the issue at hand. Take advantage of this felicitous condition.

1: Rash, impetuous action will alienate you from the larger groups to which you belong. Be conservative in the course you follow.

Unchanging: You have cut yourself off too much from contact with others. You need to get back into the circulation of humanity; go out and make friends, join groups, socialize. Learn to share your life more fully with others, mentally and emotionally as well as physically.

8. Union

There is an excellent opportunity to achieve greater unity in your relationship, whether it involves one other person or a whole group. Take time to reflect on the values, themes, and interests that have drawn you together. What do you share? How can you expand your involvement in or commitment to these concerns, and thereby strengthen the bond of the relationship? In this light, it may be helpful to reflect upon the sense of sharing and mutual exchange that first helped you build this bond. What can be done to put this sense of union back into the relationship? How can the vitality of this relationship be recharged and even expanded?

Dominant: Beware of false calls for unity—attempts by people who are not in positions of authority to try to manipulate you (and others) to do their bidding in the name of unity (family unity, corporate unity, etc.). True leaders inspire a devotion to unity; they do not coerce it. The call for unity is never made in the context of guilt.

Subordinate: If you are a leader, you have a rare opportunity to draw forth from others a deeper sense of unity and commitment. Devote yourself to understanding the purpose that unites you as well as you can, inspiring others to rally to it as well.

THE CHANGING LINES

6: Unless you are inspired by the purpose that unites everyone involved, you will miss an excellent opportunity to promote a deeper state of oneness.

5: Any effort made to increase the unity within this relationship or group will draw a favorable response.

4: The others involved respect you and are willing to rely on you. Your influence could be great, if you use it wisely.

3: Drawing closer to this individual or group would not be in your best interest. It would be an association you might regret later on.

2: Others will ask you to join them. Be sure their goals, values, and principles complement your own.

1: Your preoccupation with yourself and your limitations is preventing you from joining fully in a relationship or group. Don't be afraid to play your part!

Unchanging: You are being called upon to take a leadership position in this situation. Before accepting, however, examine your own motives to make sure they are in harmony with those of the group or the relationship. Will you be a unifying force, or a divisive one?

9. Refinement

Improvements in this relationship can only come at this point in time from the changes you make within yourself—in your own expectations, attitudes, and behavior. If you are looking for major changes to be initiated by the other person, you will be sorely disappointed—and that disappointment will only make it more difficult for the relationship to reach its full potential. Spend your time, therefore, refining your own attitudes and traits. Become more appreciative of what this other person means to you; learn to look at this relationship through his or her eyes as well as your own. You may be surprised how much of the misunderstanding or lack of agreement in this relationship has actually been caused by your own self-centered assumptions.

Dominant: If you try to throw your weight around at this time, you will find out how little weight you actually have. Do not rock the boat. It's a horrible time to pick a fight or issue ultimatums. Instead, be patient and as friendly and as agreeable as possible.

Subordinate: Avoid rash actions. Be gentle and supportive of those who rely on you. Otherwise, you may set in motion patterns you can never correct.

THE CHANGING LINES

6: Be satisfied with what you have achieved. If you become too aggressive or greedy now, you may undo all the good that has been done.
5: You can rely on the loyalty and cooperation of the others concerned. Just don't abuse it.
4: Strive for cooperation. A lot of this will depend upon your own attitudes and willingness to bend.
3: Do not underestimate the determination of others. It is silly to make enemies out of people who could easily be your friends.
2: Exercise control over your emotions. Flashes of anger or immaturity will embarrass you—and possibly even force you to withdraw.
1: You will be forced to undo the rash actions you have taken, or may be planning to take. Refraining from taking these steps in the first place would be the better policy.

Unchanging: Your desire to improve this relationship is being blocked by a misunderstanding you can not correct. If you try to make amends, you will only make the matter worse. Accept it with detachment and let time demonstrate the truth of the situation.

10. Honor

The way others view you is being tested, and the outcome will depend largely on your own sense of honor in dealing with others. In other words, do you respect the individuality and integrity of others—or do you just try to use and manipulate them for your own ends? When you make mistakes, do you blame others and try to find a convenient scapegoat? Any tendency to mistreat others in these ways will be exposed at this time. It is not their reputation, but your own, which is on the line. It is therefore important to review the ways in which you normally act, and make sure that they always express a full measure of personal honor, dignity, and respect for others.

Dominant: You may be asked to play the role of "fall guy" to save others from embarrassment. It may be better to withdraw from the situation than to play a part in such a deception.

Subordinate: It is important to respect the integrity and humanity of everyone you deal with. Refrain from the temptation of manipulating other people with guilt or fear. Treat them fairly.

THE CHANGING LINES

6: Your integrity is of a high level, but your honor and principles may be used against you, to hurt you. Proceed with great caution; do not let yourself act pigheadedly.

5: You have made assumptions that have served you well in the past, but will now get you into trouble with those closest to you. Re-examine your values.

4: As long as you are ready to act with honor, you will be protected from the opposition of others.

3: You are trying to compete with people who are out of your league—or worse yet, playing by different rules. Drop out of the running before you run into disaster.

2: Do not let yourself become absorbed in the problems of others. Help them with advice, but do not try to live their lives for them. Above all, do not try to control them or dictate to them.

1: There has never been a better time to live by the advice: "Do unto others as you would have them do unto you."

Unchanging: You are at odds on ethical issues. It will be impossible to act wisely until these issues are brought back into harmony. Make this your first priority.

51

11. Rapport

There is an unusual degree of rapport between you and the other person involved in this relationship, setting the stage for easy communications. Now is an excellent time to get to know each other better and to share your innermost thoughts, feelings, and goals. You are on the same wavelength to a remarkable degree and can therefore exchange ideas without worrying about misunderstandings. By taking the lead in expanding the rapport that exists, you can generate new opportunities for a more fruitful relationship.

Dominant: Now is an excellent time to present new ideas or proposals to superiors. To the degree that you can anticipate their needs and generate plans for meeting them, you can be especially successful.

Subordinate: Others are looking to you for guidance and support. It is of special importance at this time to be sensitive to their needs, their hurts, and their triumphs. Be liberal with praise and compliments. Seek out their opinions; incorporate them into the decision making process.

THE CHANGING LINES

6: Although outer events may not seem pleasant, they give you a reason to get to know others at a deeper, more profound level. This will put you in a good position for the future.

5: Even though you are able to understand the motives of others clearly, they are not responding to your initiatives. Redirect your efforts.

4: Chance meetings may well lead to important new opportunities. Once a line of communication is open, be sure to follow through on it.

3: It will become clear which colleagues you can work with most successfully. Be guided accordingly.

2: Use this occasion to break down some of the barriers of intolerance and bigotry that might separate you from others.

1: It is easier than normal to get along well with others. Use this occasion to build stronger cooperation and goodwill.

Unchanging: Others depend upon you to guide them wisely. If you accept the full implications of this responsibility, you will be able to create good fortune for all.

12. Impasse

This relationship has hit a roadblock, an obstacle it cannot overcome at present. In contrast to the rapport found in the last hexagram, the common wavelength that once brought this relationship into being is now producing only discord. Each party is heading in different directions, and there is little hope they will intersect again soon. There is no basis for compromise or healing at present. It is therefore best to accept the situation as it is and let it be, until the impasse no longer exists. Keep in mind that this impasse probably is not a permanent one. If you can refrain from "burning your bridges," it may be possible to pick up the relationship again at a later time. For now, it will be best to put your energies elsewhere.

Dominant: Even though this impasse is caused by natural cycles of life, you may be blamed for the deterioration that has occurred. You may be accused of being apathetic, unsupportive. If these charges are true, correct your attitudes and behavior. But if they are not, do not try to defend yourself. Hold fast to your goals and dignity.

Subordinate: There is a tremendous potential for being misunderstood by others. If you must communicate, be as clear and simple as possible. Make sure those who need to know have grasped what you said.

THE CHANGING LINES

6: You will need as much goodwill and forgiveness as you can muster to actually turn this relationship around, but it can be done.

5: The dam is about to break, and the impasse will yield to new progress. Do not throw in the towel prematurely; be patient.

4: The frustration and irritation you are experiencing result from your unwillingness to accept the "handwriting on the wall."

3: Your own ethical lapses are being called to your attention by your friends and associates. Do not blame them for problems of your own creation.

2: The impasse that has occurred is largely due to your own misplaced expectations. Adjust them.

1: There is little hope for renewed progress in this relationship. It may be best to withdraw.

Unchanging: The attempt to cling to this relationship is counterproductive, and causing you to miss new opportunities for growth. Accept what has happened, put it behind you, and get on with your life.

13. Cooperation

Whether you are dealing with one other person or a whole group, the key to success lies in greater cooperation on your part. This is not a situation where you can advance your own agenda and hope to accomplish much. Indeed, you may well need to set aside your own personal wishes and desires and yield to the needs of the relationship as a whole—what is in the best interest of everyone involved. But it is not enough just to work on behalf of everyone. It is also important to act in a way that invites others to work side by side with you. In other words, you must cultivate a genuine sense of community spirit and cooperation, in your thinking, acting, and feeling.

Dominant: Play your part in this relationship or group with goodwill, a steady commitment to mutual ideals, and cooperation, even if your role is small or seemingly unimportant. Feelings of alienation or separatism are out of place and counterproductive.

Subordinate: Resist the temptation to think of others as your personal slaves. This kind of dehumanizing attitude undermines the potential for cooperation in any relationship, and ultimately makes you look foolish.

THE CHANGING LINES

6: You may have to take a stand that will not be popular with others. Do not fight them, but be sure to draw the strength you need from your values.
5: Take care not to seek comfort in mutual complaining about the ills of society. Band together instead to implement solutions.
4: Your personal ambitions have made it hard for you to recognize the value you derive from group cooperation. It's time for a reassessment.
3: Common goals and values are in danger of being distorted—or overthrown. Unless you and others remain alert, this could happen under your noses.
2: Your need for group contact is almost a dependency. You need to consider how you can help the group instead of focusing so much on how important the group is for you.
1: This relationship brings you into contact with a group of people vital to you. Pursue this contact.

Unchanging: Do not wait for others to act. If the meaning of this bond is to deepen, you will have to make a deeper commitment to it. Offer your cooperation.

14. Eminence

On the issue at hand, you have a proper understanding of what must be done and the potential to implement it. If you act wisely, the others involved will rally around you and accept your guidance. However, do not let this moment of eminence go to your head. It is not a permanent condition. Rather, it is an opportunity to act. If you can seize this opportunity with humility and modesty, perform your duty, and then relinquish your eminence at the end of the cycle, you will have achieved much.

Dominant: It is never easy dealing with superiors whose views on important issues clash with yours. In this case, however, the authority of your ideas and recommendations will be recognized, and you will be listened to. Just do not become smug.

Subordinate: Do not act defensively about power and position—there is no need to. Inspire others to live up to their own creativity and potential and they will respond by accepting the authority of your ideas.

THE CHANGING LINES

6: If you share the eminence that comes to you with those who have helped you reach it, it will become a pattern that repeats itself throughout life.
5: Your position of eminence is based on patterns of inner purpose and relationship. Seek to serve these inner patterns, not your personal whims.
4: It would be easy to succumb to the vanity of your eminence and forget the others involved. But then they could not be depended on in the future.
3: Do not rest on the laurels of what has been accomplished. Draw in others who can help your plans develop and expand.
2: Guard against excessive pride and self-confidence. The admiration of others will not always come this easily.
1: You are blessed with many friendships. Do not take them for granted, but nurture each one.

Unchanging: You must forego personal needs and desires in order to serve the needs of this relationship—or the needs of your community.

15. Checks and Balances

The two (or more) of you in this relationship are at odds on this issue, but this should be helpful to you, not a hindrance. You both tend toward the extreme on this question—just in opposite directions. Each of you therefore has a healthy moderating influence on the other, so long as you find a way to compromise and do not come to blows. Learn to respect the differences in your points of view and appreciate the sincerity and integrity of the other person's perspectives. The key to improving this relationship lies not in reforming the other person and converting him or her to your belief, but rather in accepting him or her as an individual who enriches your life and complements your own understanding of life.

Dominant: Take care not to criticize people and decisions you do not understand. Try to support people who must make difficult choices, not second guess them.

Subordinate: Listen to the alternate points of view of those people who are in a position to help you. Do not assume that you know all the answers. Treat your subordinates with respect and you will be able to tap a pool of intelligence you have been ignoring.

THE CHANGING LINES

6: The two of you are indulging each other's immaturity. This is destructive. You both need to learn greater self-discipline.
5: Unless you learn to establish a proper balance with your own higher self, you can hardly expect to achieve harmony in this relationship.
4: Personal demands threaten the equilibrium of this relationship. It is necessary to find a way to restore harmony.
3: If you act with patience, modesty, and goodwill, you can achieve results beyond your dreams.
2: Take ownership of your share of responsibility for making this relationship work. Blaming others is unproductive. Appreciate their contributions.
1: Accept the restraints imposed upon you. They help you act more effectively in this situation.

Unchanging: Your stubbornness is an obstacle that will have to be moderated before this relationship can develop.

16. Guidance

The relationship itself is guiding you at this time, providing you with the answers you need. It is important that you take the time to listen to the clues that surround you and take them seriously. As the old cliché states it, actions do speak louder than words. Get beyond your concept of what this relationship means and evaluate what its true status is, at the present moment. Is your rapport strong—or has it been dulled? Are you appreciative of the contributions the others make—or are you critical of their errors? Is their respect for you still strong—or has it diminished? When working together, do you reach your goals easily—or does it resemble a world war? What changes must be made to heal the patterns that have arisen—or to capitalize on the enthusiasm and vitality that is generated by this bond?

Dominant: Try to understand the larger context in which this relationship exists, and the meaning it imparts. Look beyond personal needs and hurts and try to grasp the inner, impersonal reasons behind this joint effort.

Subordinate: Try to touch the chord of common interest that will inspire others to give their heart and soul to the needs at hand. You have the potential to rally great support if you act wisely.

THE CHANGING LINES

6: You are making unrealistic demands on others. Do not let your own enthusiasm become a tyrant.

5: Others may not understand you, no matter how hard you try to explain yourself. Hold to your vision of what can be done nevertheless.

4: Confidence in what you are doing will act as a strong magnet attracting others who can help you succeed.

3: Do not be swayed by the enthusiasm of others, unless it serves a genuine need for all concerned.

2: Make sure that this relationship is not just a by-product of passing fancies and needs. Tap the real human being within other people.

1: You have alienated someone of power by trying to use his or her authority for your own advancement. You need to redefine the role you are to play.

Unchanging: Outer conditions are too confusing to guide you effectively. Turn instead to the voice of the higher self and your deepest values, and let your own maturity dictate the correct steps to take.

17. Conforming

We often think of conformity in a negative sense, as being a sheep in a herd. But individuality can only grow and prosper in the larger context of society. Part of the art of enlightened action, therefore, is knowing when to accept and conform—and when to assert our selfhood. This hexagram indicates that the question at hand must be answered with a greater willingness to conform—to the rules of society, to the expectations of others, and to the patterns of life. If you keep in mind that the higher self conforms to the divine archetypal patterns and laws of life, this request for conformity should be no problem. Instead of "giving in" to the petty demands of another person, therefore, we learn to conform to the larger context which gives this relationship importance.

Dominant: Align yourself only with those leaders or guides who show an ability to conform with the realities of life. Shun those who are caught up in their own vanity and egotism.

Subordinate: You cannot achieve conformity by imposing it on others; you will only produce rebellion. You must inspire others to conform by educating them about the common goals and purposes you serve.

THE CHANGING LINES

6: Do not hide behind a wall of indifference. Be open to accepting new responsibilities for helping others grow.

5: If you look for the best within other people, you will find most of them will use it in dealing with you.

4: Your efforts to adapt are really nothing more than a thinly disguised attempt to get other people to cater to your needs. Do not succumb to self-pity.

3: It is time to part company with people who have been a drag on your own development.

2: You may think you have suffered a loss, but if you could see conditions more clearly, you would realize you have made a major gain.

1: Outer conditions are changing rapidly. Be sure to stay abreast of them; be willing to adapt.

Unchanging: No improvements can be made in this relationship until you accept full responsibility for honoring the commitments you have made. Grow up!

18. Ruin

Without ever intending to, you have let this relationship (or issue) slide into a state of disrepair, like the tumbled down ruins of a once-magnificent mansion. It is not so much what you have done that has led to this condition of ruin, but what you failed to do; you have failed to maintain and nurture the relationship, just as one might fail to maintain a building. But the structure is still sound, and can be rebuilt, if you are willing to commit yourself to a program of reconstruction. Do not overreact or initiate major changes; simply look at what you have lost and determine what should have been done to prevent it. Then develop a reasonable plan for repairing the damage. A parent, for example, might realize that his or her preoccupation with other issues of life has led to a state of ruin in his or her parental relationship. The fault here lies not with the child but with the parent, and must be corrected not through punishment but renewed effort to nurture the growth of the child.

Dominant: You have become obsessed with personal problems and have neglected to serve the larger purpose of this relationship. Get back on track before it is too late.

Subordinate: You have ignored your duties to care for and nurture the others concerned. Do not let this situation continue to slide into ruin.

THE CHANGING LINES

6: You are not responsible for the ruin that has occurred. Therefore, the best contribution you can make is to focus on the larger perspective and become an agent of goodwill.

5: You've let moral issues interfere with your relationship. Don't be so self-righteous. Accept others for what they are, not what you want them to be.

4: As long as the changes you strive to make are consistent with your deepest values, your efforts to rebuild will bring good fortune.

3: You have a good grasp of the changes that must be made. Fill yourself with the courage to make them, in spite of resistance from other quarters.

2: In your zeal to correct past mistakes you have made, you have unwittingly hurt or threatened others. Make amends before it is too late.

1: It is not the relationship that is stifling you, but the context in which you approach it. You need to change your own basic assumptions to clear the air.

Unchanging: The problem lies not just in this one relationship; a number of your bonds with others are rapidly approaching ruin. People are tired of indulging you. You need expert help to reverse this trend.

19. Blossoming

Your relationship is about to blossom, either because it is a new one or because favorable conditions will revitalize it. This is therefore a good time to make overtures to expand the scope of the relationship, or to discover a level of richness you have previously overlooked. The key to acting at this time is to nurture the best elements within this relationship. Always remember that while the blossoms of spring are filled with optimism and hope, the tree only reaches fulfillment in late summer, when the fruit has fully matured. There is great promise at this point, but much hard work will be required to realize the full potential of this relationship. It is therefore important to use the time of blossoming to build a foundation of caring, respect, and appreciation for the others involved.

Dominant: Now is the time to present innovative ideas to those in authority. In general, a tremendous opportunity exists to improve your ties with those who direct or supervise you.

Subordinate: As you bring new people under your wing, remember that they do not share the same level of commitment and enthusiasm as you. Give them time to blossom according to their own talents.

THE CHANGING LINES

6: Your own progress can become the basis for the blossoming of talent in others, if you are willing to reinvest your gains in them.
5: Be sure to share the joy and triumph of this time with others. Give full credit to the contributions of your colleagues.
4: This situation is rich with blessings. Do not be reluctant to accept them wholeheartedly.
3: Do not misread the signals coming from others. Excessive enthusiasm is often very short-lived.
2: Build this relationship on a solid foundation. Do not approach it as an escape into fantasy or selfish fulfillment.
1: This relationship has rich potential. Make the effort to cultivate it and help it blossom.

Unchanging: There is a special potential within this relationship which compels you to discover it and help it unfold. Do not shirk from this task; it will enrich your life greatly.

20. Activating the Ideal

Within every situation of life, there is an ideal way of acting and thinking, as determined by the higher self. There is an ideal for you as a parent, a lover, a student, a teacher, an employee, a boss, or a friend. There are even ideals for specific situations, such as when an aging parent treats you like a child even though you are now an adult. You are in a situation where it is imperative to activate the ideal and express it through your relationship. This process consists of three steps: contemplating the ideal and becoming familiar with it, conceiving a way to express this ideal in the day-to-day interactions of this relationship, and then making sure you do express it when the opportunity arises. Do not wait for the others involved to start acting ideally, however; you must be the agent through which this ideal is expressed.

Dominant: Accept the guidance of those with more experience than you gratefully, for there is much you can learn from them if you are on their wavelength.

Subordinate: Others are looking to you for guidance. Take the time to provide it. Welcome their openness.

THE CHANGING LINES

6: Do not become so caught up in the ideal that you forget to express it in practical ways. This relationship is teaching you to activate what you know.

5: Contemplation of the ideal brings wisdom, enabling you to reestablish this relationship on a whole new level. You can now become aware of some of the inner dynamics of this bond.

4: From the perspective of the ideal, you can see more accurately how this relationship should develop. Use this insight wisely.

3: Until you are able to forgive, you will be unable to grasp the spiritual ideal governing this relationship. You condemn yourself to repeating the problem.

2: You have a good feel for the situation—but unfortunately your feelings have misled you. You need to learn to serve and love the ideal.

1: Your understanding of this situation is severely limited by your own assumptions and prejudices. Open yourself up to a higher perspective.

Unchanging: If you share your insights into the ideal with the others involved, you will discover a rich new basis for mutual expression.

21. Intimidation

You have allowed someone else to establish a level of dominance or influence over you that is decidedly unhealthy, and now they are taking advantage of it by intimidating you. This can range all the way from psychological blackmail on the one hand to the clever manipulation of your fears and anxieties on the other. In any event, it is dangerous to allow this situation to continue, lest you get completely swallowed up in this pattern. But the answer does not lie in fighting fire with fire. Do not make an enemy of this person. Understand that it was your own blindness or short-sightedness which allowed this situation to fester. Eliminate all tendencies toward manipulating others in yourself, and then take the second step of cutting off their influence over you. Close the doors by which they have been manipulating you.

Dominant: Attempts to undermine the position of those who are responsible for your well-being are stupid and short-sighted. These people are meant to be your allies, not your enemies.

Subordinate: You have been building relationships in order to have scapegoats. This is a good way to lose friends in a hurry; you need to put a stop to it.

THE CHANGING LINES

6: If you give in to this intimidation, you condemn yourself to further suffering and evil.

5: Do not allow yourself to be blackmailed psychologically any more. Accept whatever losses may occur, and start over again.

4: You have lost power to another only because you willingly gave it up. Learn to rely on your inner strength, and you will be able to overcome this threat of intimidation.

3: You have trapped yourself in a maze of your own confusion and misunderstanding. Others have now moved in, to prey on your self-created chaos.

2: Your disappointment in another is only a mirror image of your disappointment in yourself.

1: You are being given an object lesson. Change your methods of treating others, before it is too late.

Unchanging: It is your own guilty conscience that is intimidating you, not other people. You need to clean up your own mental household before you can expect to deal honestly with others.

22. Skin Deep

The relationship in question seems to be a good one, for it has brought you enjoyment, but it is not based on a solid foundation of values and common interests. It is a rather superficial bond, based more on personal charm and mutual attraction than anything enduring. Once the needs of the moment have passed, the relationship will probably be discarded and forgotten. It certainly does not have the strength to endure any real conflict—or growth. Enjoy it while it lasts, but do not rely on it to make any substantial contribution to your life. Look for deeper, more genuine levels of satisfaction elsewhere.

Dominant: You have benefitted greatly from effective public relations and a good first impression. But the time is rapidly approaching when you will have to prove your worth in more substantial ways. Make sure you are ready.

Subordinate: Don't be caught off guard by the idol worship of someone who looks up to you. It could well set you up for an embarrassing disappointment.

THE CHANGING LINES

6: You are not dealing with other people as humans; you deal with them as cartoon characters. Learn to relate to others at a more enduring level.
5: You have tried to pass yourself off as someone you are not. As a result, you may never be treated as the person you really are.
4: This situation is setting you up for a major let-down.
3: You have a tendency to evaluate people in very superficial ways. Put more faith in qualities of character than possessions and appearances.
2: You are under the influence of some major glamours about life. Come down off of cloud nine.
1: The attraction you are feeling is mostly skin deep. It may be fun, but it is unlikely to develop into something substantial.

Unchanging: You have adopted something of a Pollyannish approach to life, and this has blinded you to the flaws and weaknesses of others. Idealism is a virtue, but immaturity is not.

23. Unraveling

The bond that has brought you together is in the process of rapidly unraveling. Unless a way can be found to renew the relationship with a fresh sense of purpose, the tie may well come apart completely. It will not be easy to find a way to restore the bond, however, because the flow of energies is toward dissolution. In many cases, it may be best just to accept this decay, and move on to new chapters in your life. In others, however, it would be a shame to allow a strong and meaningful bond to come apart in this fashion. In these instances, it is best to keep a low profile, making sure you do nothing to aggravate the problem. Wait for a time when it will be easier to clear up misunderstandings and answer wrongful accusations. In the interim, nourish the relationship with affection, goodwill, and understanding.

Dominant: The temptation to rebel against people who do not seem to understand you is great. Yet if you do, you will cause far greater damage than you realize. Be restrained.

Subordinate: There comes a time when the young must leave the nest. Do not try to prevent it; accept it with grace and loving support. Make sure they take your blessing with them, be this a family, an academic, or a business setting.

THE CHANGING LINES

6: Keep a low profile; do not overreact to the threat to this relationship. Unless you feed it unwisely, the threat may well pass without major damage.
5: A relationship that unraveled a long time ago can now be healed. Extend forgiveness and a willingness to reconcile.
4: The unraveling of this relationship is in your own best interest, as it will open up new opportunities for growth.
3: Learn what you can from your mistakes, so that you will not have to repeat this situation.
2: You have played your part in undermining this relationship. Self-pity will not solve your problem.
1: There is nothing you can do to stop the unraveling of this relationship. Let go.

Unchanging: Accept the inevitable as gracefully as possible. Do not get caught up in cycles of blame or guilt; get busy creating new opportunities.

24. The Rebound

Whenever situations unravel completely, as indicated in hexagram 23, life immediately begins to rebound. New beginnings become inevitable. But are they new beginnings, or just the start of the same old patterns as before? If we have learned and grown as a result of our experiences, they will be true new beginnings. But if we are rebounding just because the movement of life forces us to, we can be sure we are recycling the same patterns as before. It is therefore important at this stage to examine new relationships, or new cycles in established ones. What is the purpose and the potential of this bond? How can it enrich our life? What are we meant to contribute to it? What are we learning from it? How can we avoid repeating the mistakes of the past?

Dominant: It can be very illuminating to examine what kind of people we end up being subservient to. Are they kind and generous in their dealings with us? Or harsh and critical? What does this tell us about ourself?

Subordinate: In the same way, how do we habitually treat people who are dependent on us? As a petty tyrant? As a nurturing parent? What does this tell us about ourself?

THE CHANGING LINES

6: You are in danger of becoming misanthropic, shutting others out of your life. Reverse this trend before it becomes set.
5: You have forgotten how to make new friends. Do not be so absorbed in yourself.
4: Do not be afraid to make new friends. They will lead you into new worlds, new interests.
3: It is understandable that you may be uncertain what to do. Trust in your higher self to guide you and launch you on new cycles of development.
2: Seek out relationships in which you can invest your goodwill, helpfulness, and friendship.
1: During times of rebounding, you may be tempted to strike up relationships that would be less than ideal. Exercise caution; take care of yourself.

Unchanging: You have begun to think of yourself as a pawn of Fate, passively accepting whatever comes to you without making much effort to direct it or control it. This is not desirable. You have spun the patterns of Fate yourself, and only you can write a better, more fulfilling script.

79

25. Unexpected Events

Some people plan every detail of their lives, including their relationships. Others are more spontaneous and free in their actions; they have overall goals, but are able to respond quickly to new opportunities as they arise. They are also able to enjoy whatever experiences life arranges for them. In the present situation, it would be counterproductive to try to program a specific result. Be relaxed and let this relationship develop its own momentum. In fact, if it has begun to stagnate, do something unexpected. Attune yourself with the momentum within the relationship, and let it determine the next few steps to take.

Dominant: Welcome unexpected requests or commands, even though they may seem like unwanted burdens at first. If you respond well to these requests, they may well lead to broader horizons.

Subordinate: Do not try to regimentize those who are subordinate to you, whether in a family or the workplace. Respect the individuality of each and treat each one as a unique human being.

THE CHANGING LINES

6: Your actions are driving away support rather than attracting it. Calm down and relax until a better opportunity arises.

5: You will be criticized for rocking the boat. Hold fast to your creative vision, and let the boat rock!

4: Shun gossip. Do not let others adversely influence your opinion of other people, especially friends.

3: People you rely on may prove unreliable. Before criticizing them, however, try to understand why they have behaved so unpredictably.

2: Scheming, manipulation, and efforts to curry the favor of important people will all backfire. Treat others honestly and fairly.

1: Do not force yourself to live up to someone else's expectations. It's enough of a job to be yourself.

Unchanging: Unexpected changes will put this situation in an entirely new light. Be flexible and willing to accommodate changes that are in the best interest of everyone involved.

26. Expanding Influence

A tremendous amount of energy is available that will enable you to expand your sphere of influence. Especially in interpersonal relationships, it will now be possible to communicate more effectively, win support, and inspire the thinking and actions of others. You may well make new friends, or find it possible to revive old ties that have become estranged. The key, as always, is to focus on the mutual interests you share with others. As you expand your involvement in these pursuits, you will find others gathering around you to help. It will be the power of your ideas, values, and motivation that attracts them, rather than your personal charm. Use this power with restraint, however, for the damage it could do would be tremendous if it should be unleashed in petty ways.

Dominant: You may well be overwhelmed by the intensity of power expressed by someone else—in a moment of anger, a quick reprimand, or a flash of frustration. Do not overreact. This power is also being directed creatively, and you are benefitting.

Subordinate: Stick with the common activity that brings you all together. If you let the group be distracted by petty problems, the great opportunity of this moment may be lost for all.

THE CHANGING LINES

6: The sphere of influence that has been created is more important than any one individual, even you. Serve it wisely and you will prosper.
5: To take full advantage of your expanding influence you must submit to the guidance of your own higher self.
4: Opposition yields rapidly before you—perhaps too rapidly. Take nothing for granted.
3: New doors are opening, and you are meeting new faces to go with them. Each new situation creates a choice. Rely on your values as you choose.
2: Accept the limitations of this situation. Do not respond with anger, lest you destroy something of great value to you.
1: There will be rapid movement forward in opportunity, but the time is not yet ripe. Be patient.

Unchanging: The energies that have been unleashed are too explosive to be handled with control. You will have to ease off until the pressure has been released.

27. Right Investment

What you put into a relationship is what you will get back out of it, and the situation at hand is an excellent measure of what you have been investing in this bond. The wise person invests affection, helpfulness, goodwill, and patience. He does not criticize, but lovingly helps his friend see where he has erred. He does not embarrass others; he supports them. He does not try to manipulate them; he respects their integrity. As a result, he is helped and supported in return. All too many people, however, have failed to learn this lesson. They mistreat their friends and loved ones, by harshly criticizing them, humiliating them, and blackmailing them emotionally. By studying conditions in the situation at hand, you can see fairly easily what kind of investment you have been making. How should it be adjusted?

Dominant: You are called on to be a helper in this situation. You can resent it, and make this role undignified. Or you can see the great value of being a helper, and make it a creative opportunity.

Subordinate: You are called on to nourish the growth and competence of others. This is a great responsibility, calling forth the full measure of your love, wisdom, and strength. Do not underplay the value of this role.

THE CHANGING LINES

6: Your efforts to help others have taught you much about goodwill. You can now use it to serve wisely as opportunity arises.

5: You are focusing on what is wrong in this relationship and have let criticism take over. Give more time to reflecting on what is good and making it work again.

4: In spite of criticism from some quarters, your efforts to help are very much appreciated—and useful.

3: Jealousy is a viper that poisons any relationship in which it occurs. Take care not to engage in it.

2: There is a great opportunity to expand your capacity to be a true helper in this situation.

1: It is not necessary to become a martyr; just learn to nurture the best within each friend and loved one.

Unchanging: You have succumbed to the idea that "you care too much." This is warping your values. No one cares too much, although some people do develop a martyr complex, where they expect recognition for caring and loving. This is a problem of too much self-pity, not too much love. Change your attitudes before you fall in love with being a victim.

28. The Onslaught

Issues and pressures have been building for some time, and now the dam is bursting. Suddenly, it is as though everyone is against you, including friends and loved ones you thought you could count on. Of course, they are still with you—they are just giving you advice you don't want to hear. This is a time of crisis and opportunity. The risk is high, because if you behave petulantly, you may alienate friends and colleagues. But the reward can also be high, because if you sense the opportunities for change and growth, you may be able to make substantial forward progress. For this reason, do not respond defensively or adversely to the suggestions of friends and loved ones. Listen to what they are saying, and in it, look for clues as to how you should act. Treasure their support and help, even if it seems to come in a form that you would normally reject. Take the time of onslaught to deepen your friendships, not scuttle them. Recognize your friends as one of your greatest assets of living.

Dominant: Do not reject the advice of people who seem to be ganging up against you. It has taken some courage for them to come together to warn you of the danger they see. Respect their sincerity.

Subordinate: You cannot delegate responsibility for handling a crisis to others. This is your crisis; you must face it directly.

THE CHANGING LINES

6: The onslaught is passing. It is time to be grateful for the help of those who proved to be true friends.
5: It is important to be true to your ideals, but it is also important to preserve useful friendships. Be practical in your actions now, so that you can preserve your outer connections as well as your inner ones.
4: You must take your stand against the onslaught as you see fit. Those who support you will stand with you; do not worry about the rest.
3: You are misconstruing helpful advice as insults. You need to develop a greater faith in your friends.
2: People you normally view as inexperienced may be able to assist you better than established experts.
1: You have wasted valuable time blaming the very people you ought to be heeding. It's time to discover your true friends.

Unchanging: It may seem necessary to act alone at this time of onslaught. But when the dust has cleared, you will be aware that you have had a great deal of support. Do not be blind to this, even if it is not readily apparent.

29. The Trap

A weakness within your character is leading you further and further into a relationship which is not good for you—and is, in fact, a trap that will be very hard to extricate yourself from. Greed, for example, could drive you to form a partnership with a highly unethical person, who leaves you holding the bag when your shady empire comes crashing down. A need to dominate others might drive you into marrying a very weak person who becomes a far greater burden than you ever bargained for—and, who, by his or her weakness, ends up dominating you! This trap is already in the process of being formed, but keep in mind that your greatest problem is not the trap, but rather the weakness in your own character that consistently leads you into this trap.

Dominant: You are being set up to take the fall for someone else. Do not fight this openly; let your own integrity be your defense. But it may be wise to shift allegiances.

Subordinate: You have cried wolf once too often. Now, at a time of real danger, no one will take your calls for help seriously. You will have to face this threat on your own.

THE CHANGING LINES

6: You have succumbed to the trap inherent in this relationship. There is nothing you can do except wait to be released.

5: Do not overreact to the danger at hand, lest you deepen your difficulties.

4: The way out of your trap is a simple one. Do not make it any more complex than it has to be.

3: Your thinking is being influenced by strong people who are using you as a pawn. It may become necessary to withdraw from the situation.

2: You are caught in the snare of your own defensiveness. The only way you can redeem yourself is by small, cautious steps that will prove your worth.

1: You have associated too much with people with dubious values. Their situational ethics have blurred your own sense of propriety, leaving you trapped in confusion.

Unchanging: Your psychological abuse of others has become a trap you cannot escape—until you learn the value of treating others with respect, friendship, and support.

30. Dependency

Our modern concern about dependency in relationships is a bit overdone. All relationships involve a two-way dependency; to some degree, each person depends on the other to carry his or her share of the load. Without dependency, there is no relationship. But like any good thing when carried to excess, dependency can cause problems if it gets out of balance. If we lean on others too much to do our work for us, we lose our independence, and the viability of the relationship suffers. In the situation at hand, this delicate balance has been abused. We need to examine it carefully and try to determine what adjustments will help restore proper proportion to our lives.

Dominant: You are clinging too much to a mentor or role model. Instead of creating your own style, you are just imitating this person (or group). You need to stop idolizing this hero and develop your own way of thinking and doing things. Express your Self—not someone else!

Subordinate: You are holding on too much to people who need to get out on their own. Your responsibility for them is fulfilled; now it is time for you to retire into the background and give them center stage. Let them be themselves.

THE CHANGING LINES

6: You have cultivated a victim consciousness, yet you are primarily a victim of your own self-deception. Stop defeating yourself; find the power within you that can triumph.
5: You misunderstand the situation. You are more caught up in your own self-pity than in learning to deal with others honestly and fairly.
4: You are blinding yourself with euphoria. You may be overcommitting yourself in this situation.
3: Do not be afraid to accept help from others when you need it. The self-reliant person also knows when to accept assistance.
2: A good balance between strengths and weaknesses exists in this relationship. Good fortune will come from nurturing it.
1: You are not yet ready to fly on your own. You need the protective help of being dependent on another for guidance and understanding.

Unchanging: When there is imbalance in our relationship, there is inevitably imbalance in our own character. We are at war with ourself. Our need is to cultivate better inner health, so that we will be able to relate more openly with others.

31. Openness

As the poet John Donne put it, "No man is an island unto himself." We cannot live behind the walls of defensiveness, estrangement, and paranoia; we need contacts with other people, through family, work, and social activities. To strike up meaningful relationships, however, we must be open and responsive to others; we must let them into our lives. We must let them interact with our feelings, our thoughts, our goals, and even our values—to different degrees, of course, depending upon the level of intimacy. When this hexagram comes up, it suggests that you need to establish a greater level of openness in this relationship. Get to know the others involved as human beings—not just as your concept of who they are. Let them get to know you. To whatever degree possible, share your inner life with them.

Dominant: You have treated this person (or group) somewhat superstitiously, ascribing to him powers and influences that he does not possess. There is too much fear in your reaction to this individual. This needs to be corrected.

Subordinate: You are far too defensive to the challenges of others. They are not trying to bite your head off. Relax and loosen up a bit. Learn to cooperate with their ideas and suggestions more openly.

THE CHANGING LINES

6: If you take the initiative, you can tap a measure of enduring joy.

5: There is an unusual opportunity to build a profound level of rapport in this relationship.

4: Clever schemes will backfire in your face, forcing you to become defensive—which will embarrass you further.

3: Your best course of action is to be open and direct. Lay your cards on the table and let the others respond as they see fit.

2: The satisfaction and fulfillment you are experiencing are real; this is not a dream.

1: You are too open and easy-going. Some of the people you associate with will take advantage of you, unless you become more discerning.

Unchanging: Progress can only be made by sharing the joys and the burdens of this activity together. It is time to deepen the level of your affection.

32. Traditional Roles

One of the great problems in many modern relationships is the confusion that has arisen as society's traditional roles have been questioned, updated, and sometimes discarded. Most of this revision has been healthy, but some of it has left many people perplexed. There is value in the traditional roles, which is why they became traditions; nonetheless, anything that becomes too rigid loses its usefulness. There is some confusion in your current situation about traditional roles and how they are to be performed. This is something that needs to be worked out by everyone concerned, in a way that everyone can be comfortable with. It may be helpful to remember that many of these roles are almost archetypal in nature: the loving parent, the dutiful child, the wise teacher, and so on. The key to working with traditional roles in our daily relationships is to try to capture as much of the inner meaning of this role as possible.

Dominant: When people in dominant positions fail to exercise the authority that is traditionally theirs, we may build up a measure of resentment—a feeling that we have been let down. Do not let such feelings fester.

Subordinate: Your own inner guidance is the best source of understanding how to act in roles in which you must exercise authority and responsibility.

THE CHANGING LINES

6: You are trying to be all things to all men. Let the natural roles of life focus your energies more productively.
5: Do not scorn the opportunity to play a public role of importance. Much good can result.
4: You are rebelling against these roles more to draw attention to yourself than out of sincere protest. You need to redefine the purposes of each role you play.
3: You are hiding yourself behind a role, rather than expressing your humanity through it.
2: You're putting too much pressure on others to conform to your expectations. Lighten up.
1: Your prejudice is showing. Be more open and tolerant.

Unchanging: You need to be a steady influence during times of change and development. Hold fast to your values, and thereby become an excellent example for others.

33. Disengagement

Your authority and influence in this relationship are limited; you are producing disharmony and conflict more than anything else. The best course of action is to keep contact to a minimum or withdraw entirely for the moment and wait for better times. Only small efforts and modest moves are possible now. Strict detachment may be essential to control possible resentment or fear. Your own misguided expectations—or desire to be in control—may be the cause of this conflict. Study your reactions and view this conflict as an opportunity to grow in self-understanding, self-sufficiency, and self-control.

Dominant: You may have misunderstood the potential or purpose of this relationship as well as the person. Cut your losses and retreat for now or you may find the conflict will increase. Concentrate on preventing further deterioration and on reinforcing your strengths by being more aligned to your ideals and basic values.

Subordinate: You may have expected too much from this relationship. Your influence is unwelcome now and will be rejected if you persist, making a difficult situation even worse. Curb your emotional involvement and resist the temptation to be forceful or react with worry or anger.

THE CHANGING LINES

6: Your best fortune and happiness lies in complete withdrawal from this relationship. You may do so easily and without dishonor.
5: Avoid further indecision, useless wrangling, or discussion. Withdraw from this relationship decisively and on friendly terms if possible.
4: Choose the time to withdraw carefully; then do so without regret or guilt so that you are emotionally prepared for new and better things.
3: You are being held back by elements of fear, guilt, or exaggerated responsibility. Review the validity of these sentiments.
2: You lack the determination to do what is necessary to remove yourself from this association. Gather your courage or seek those who can help you escape.
1: You have waited too long for painless retreat. Your only option is to hold your ground for now.

Unchanging: There is a steady and dominant element of disharmony in this relationship. Your only realistic course is to withdraw emotionally and physically and look for the lesson in this conflict.

34. Great Authority

The two tests of character are times of weakness and times of great power. This is a time when you will have a very strong influence on those around you. People may seek you out or pay unusual attention to your ideas and example. Others may recognize that they are depending on you. It is vital to act with great caution and discretion. Your long term well-being is dependent on building good relationships now. Seek to be in harmony with traditions and your ideals. Realize that what you do now will have major consequences long after your time of great authority has passed.

Dominant: Do not assume this period of great authority validates all of your beliefs and convictions or makes any major move less risky. You have the power to succeed or to fail in a spectacular way. Beware impulsiveness or unorthodox moves. Act with caution and seek to align yourself with major traditions. Use this time of greater influence to contribute to the needs of others.

Subordinate: Others may recognize how much they need you now. Beware the temptation to control or exploit the weakness of others. This is a time to act responsibly and play a supportive role. Let your ideals guide you. Play a traditional role in order to avoid serious misunderstanding later on.

THE CHANGING LINES

6: Part of your problem is that you have pushed your authority and influence in this relationship too far and your moves have become counterproductive.

5: Your egotism and pride are getting in the way of effective communication. Stop pushing and start listening.

4: Your best results now can be achieved by a modest style and pace. This will create a natural harmony and dissolve potential defensiveness.

3: Acting modestly and behind the scenes will permit you to be successful, while an overt show of authority will attract suspicion or opposition.

2: If you take advantage of people now because they seem so cooperative, they may resent it later.

1: You may have the power to act, but not correctly. If you use your authority now, failure may result. Rethink your plans.

Unchanging: It is absolutely essential that you give highest priority to being correct in your behavior. Take time to carefully redefine your purpose and your role in this relationship. Self-serving action will lead to disaster.

35. Influence

If you work from an intelligent and moral position, this can be a time when you can be recognized as a person of authority. Because of this, you can exert a great influence on others and increase cooperation, respect, and loyalty. However, your influence will depend on your ability to identify and develop those interests and needs you have in common with others. It is important, therefore, to establish and sustain harmony with those who can support or oppose you. Be mindful of the traditions that govern the situation. The times favor intelligent initiatives and forthright action on your part.

Dominant: Study the habits, values, and needs of this person or group so you can discern where you have common values and needs. By serving these interests, you attract favorable attention and gain support.

Subordinate: While it may be easy to manipulate others, you must avoid exploitation. Your enduring success depends on your integrity and ability to honor the values of others. Seek guidance from the traditions which govern this issue.

THE CHANGING LINES

6. The key to a better relationship lies more in changing your thinking and expectations than in changing others.

5: This is a time to practice self-control and to be magnanimous. Let the keynote be benevolence rather than personal gain.

4: There is danger of self-deception and opportunism. Be guided by your ideals.

3: Do only what will preserve and promote the greater harmony and support of all parties involved.

2: You are missing some vital information about your own motives or the party in question. Study the situation further.

1: You need to work on promoting better public relations to attract favorable attention. Sincerity and warmth will serve you well.

Unchanging: Your position of authority and quality is recognized and you can act confidently. Use this time to build on these strengths by increasing your understanding of this relationship and doing what is effective and proper.

36. Restraint

This is a time for self-restraint. Anything you say or do is likely to be misinterpreted or backfire. Despite the fact that you have a clear understanding of your values and what you want to do, you may need to "go along to get along" for the moment. This is not a matter of capitulation to the inferior as much as it is a realistic adjustment to external forces more powerful than you. Your best approach, if you must act, is to appear agreeable and compliant. Avoid any direct discussion or challenge to the ideas or behavior of others, because it will most likely evoke misunderstanding, animosity, and retaliation. You may have to accept the fact that there are major differences between you and others; little can be done to resolve them.

Dominant: Restrain any overt challenge to others; they will not be receptive to your thinking. If conflict has already occurred, try to stop it by appearing benign, agreeable, and inconspicuous. In this way you can avoid additional trouble and preserve your strength.

Subordinate: Resist the urge to force your views on others in this situation, lest it estrange you further from your goals. Hold to your ideals and plans until times are more favorable for discussion or action.

THE CHANGING LINES

6: The conflict you are experiencing and those who caused it are both in the process of self-destruction. Hold on for the moment.

5: While your views and intentions are correct, you are not able to act effectively right now. Wait for better times.

4: This situation is deteriorating. Be detached. Withdraw if possible or you may get caught in the collapse.

3: You have an opportunity to confront adversaries now. Use your power carefully or you may meet with powerful rejection.

2: Use your problem or loss to help you find added meaning to life and an incentive to help self or others.

1: Unless you endure this conflict unselfishly, you may endanger your reputation and your future.

Unchanging: Even though your attitude and intentions are correct, there is little you can do other than accept this person or group for what they are. Practice patience and self-restraint in how you respond to them.

37. Proper Conduct

The key to establishing a good relationship now is to understand the conduct expected of you by others. If your relationship is based on honesty, loyalty, and cooperation, then it will be successful. If you misunderstand your role or conduct yourself in a way that is unfair or unrealistic, you will meet with adversity. This issue cannot be decided by whim, persuasion, or artful deception. Phoniness and the effort to manipulate or dazzle others will backfire now. Rely on your values and common sense plus tradition to suggest the proper conduct for this situation. Play that role with consistency, dignity, and affection. You can then promote harmony and gain favorable attention.

Dominant: Study the stronger or more authoritative person or group to recognize exactly where cooperation can bring benefit to you. Defer to them on this basis. The qualities of loyalty, affection, sincerity, and reliability are now rewarded.

Subordinate: Look to tradition and your own strengths to help you find your natural role and conduct in this relationship. Be ready to go the extra mile to gain respect and cooperation. To be perceived as a trustworthy friend, you will have to prove it by acting like one.

THE CHANGING LINES

6: You are in a favorable position to express your wisdom, love, and talents. Gracefully accept your responsibility to do this, and you will gain respect.
5: By being charitable and generous, you establish and sustain a relationship full of trust and affection.
4: Success depends on deferring to the legitimate needs of others. Focus your attention on how you can be helpful.
3: The relationship is unbalanced or underdeveloped and needs to be rescued from its present state. Strive for a more moderate course between excessive control and permissiveness.
2: Do not be controlled by your own self-interest. Conduct yourself with respect for others in order to achieve and maintain harmony.
1: Take time to clarify the roles you and others play and the ground rules for them. This will prevent subsequent arguments and misunderstandings.

Unchanging: Seek to understand the nature of your responsibility to this person or group. The more you understand and consistently play the appropriate role, the more effective and powerful you become.

38. Disharmony

Your perception of the situation is more polarized than clear, and disharmony seems to dominate your thoughts and attitudes. This is not a time to be impatient or forceful. Perhaps you have failed to see that your differences with others are more complementary than antagonistic. Or the problem may lie in your own indecisiveness and your mixed feelings about others. Progress can be achieved as you review your own attitudes and goals. Look beyond your immediate well being and search for a larger purpose and perspective which can best serve your long term interests. You may need to embrace ideas and philosophies you have previously scorned.

Dominant: Don't be blinded by what appears to be contrasting interests and views. Review your attitudes about authority. Avoid either extreme of defensiveness or capitulation. Give top priority to promoting friendship and trust rather than arguing issues.

Subordinate: The problem may be distrust and misunderstanding more than actual conflict. Work on being more understanding and flexible. Progress may come as you reduce your self-importance and attempt only small initiatives or changes.

THE CHANGING LINES

6: You may have seriously misjudged the motives and character of others. Exercise caution and patience until you can see more clearly.

5: More than anything else, it is your own cynicism that prevents the cooperation you seek. Little will change until you do!

4: Search for one whom you trust to make sense of your confusion. This can be a wise person or your own higher self.

3: It will be essential to consult your deepest values and principles to work out a new and more realistic approach to this situation.

2: Serendipity and intuition may provide more help than logic can. Look for something unexpected to provide valuable insights or assistance.

1: Hold fast to your ideals, but otherwise don't try to fix this situation. Just wait for it to clear up on its own.

Unchanging: You seem to be in direct opposition to others and a stalemate is present. These differences run deep and will not be easily resolved. Your best hope is to work on cultivating respect for each other despite your differences. Tolerate to be tolerated.

39. Friction

Not everyone is on our wavelength or is our friend. Friction with others is bound to occur, and when it does, it occurs for one of three reasons: they cause it, we cause it, or we both cause it. In this situation, the cause is largely of your own making, and you should consider the matter a learning experience more than a handicap. Therefore, there is need to take inventory of your habits, motives, and attitudes to find the culprit. Perhaps you need to gather strength, build up your coping skills, be more creative, or more patient. This review may involve some painful confrontation with the truth or much frustration until you overcome your rationalizations and prejudices.

Dominant: It is time for you to act with greater skill than forcefulness and more accommodation than confrontation. You may need the advice and support of more experienced people to help you discern your best course.

Subordinate: Don't expect others to change much. Matters will improve to the degree that you make most of the changes. Seek out new strategies and attitudes as well as a modification in the role you play.

THE CHANGING LINES

6: It will become necessary to do more to understand and repair this relationship. Seek the counsel of those who have faced similar problems.

5: The friction in this relationship is designed to force you to consult and cooperate with the plan of your higher self. Do not resist this summons.

4: Your understanding of the relationship is too one-sided. Seek the help of others or of your higher self to expand your awareness and assist you.

3: You may be overreacting to this situation. Review your principles and real interests to put this relationship into a more valid perspective.

2: The relationship should not be abandoned. Instead, seek to work with it more creatively; invest more energy into it.

1: Exercise caution and patience until the time is more favorable for your action.

Unchanging: The restrictions in this relationship may seem to be due to others or lack of opportunity, but they really stem from your own attitudes and behavior. They may lie in your inhibitions, lack of skill, or your negative outlook. Only you can resolve these issues.

40. Clearing the Air

This is a time when you have the opportunity to clear up old misunderstandings, resolve conflicts, and make amends. The opportunity will be missed, however, unless you act with vigor and self-control. Do not wait for others to start this process; show initiative. It is time to set aside old fears, doubts, grief, and resentments. Be ready to adapt, give up the desire for retribution, modify your standards and expectations, forgive, and forget. If the situation is hopeless, perhaps this will be a time for a complete break and a new beginning. In any case, if you seize this opportunity, it will clear the way for a fresh start in this relationship and the growth of your character.

Dominant: Don't let the past blind you to the opportunity to bring new life into this relationship. Seek a new agenda that leaves out most of the past. Be guided by whatever respect you have for the good potential in the present situation; give less attention to fixing the past.

Subordinate: The situation calls for a major adjustment in your attitude about this relationship. You will find others are now more receptive to friendly and constructive overtures from you. Find a healthier way to deal with them and do so quickly.

THE CHANGING LINES

6: With great courage and skill, you can defeat an old adversary. This could be a destructive habit in you.
5: The opportunity for improvement begins in you as you shake off old fears, despair, or self-doubts. This change will precede all other potential changes.
4: Redefine your needs and responsibilities. Eliminate unnecessary duties and relationships.
3: Your authority and the control you assume are under challenge. Modify your plans and style before you lose the respect of others.
2: The selfishness of others may need to be challenged now. If you are to be constructive, stick to the issues rather than your personal feelings.
1: Take advantage of recent changes. Work quickly to capture this momentum by building on these new opportunities.

Unchanging: Powerful internal changes are occurring to rid you of habits that have blocked your progress. Focus your attention on mental house-cleaning rather than fighting adversaries. The adjustment may be painful, but it will produce enduring growth of your character.

41. Declining Potential

This relationship has entered a phase of decline. This may only be temporary and eventually could lead to a new beginning. In the meantime, it will be essential to adjust to the declining potential in the current situation. If you persist in frustrated efforts to make things happen your way, you may only aggravate the situation. You also may exhaust yourself and jeopardize the future of this relationship. It is essential to simplify your approach, lower your expectations, and withdraw somewhat for the moment. Restrain your desire to control others. Turn your attention toward self-improvement; learn to be more self-sufficient at the emotional and physical levels.

Dominant: It is time to appreciate that others are working on their agenda and at their own pace and style. You will have to allow them that privilege. Be gracious. Reduce your expectations and leave them alone.

Subordinate: Your desire to discuss issues and help is not what others seem to want. The more you try to fix things, the further you may drive them away. It will be better to work at being a patient, benevolent, and reassuring friend.

THE CHANGING LINES

6: Your recent experiences should lead to an expansion of your awareness. Look to where you can help others and be helped by them.

5: The current situation is a natural part of your destiny and cannot be avoided. By being more aligned to your higher self, you will succeed.

4: Your own reactions and frustrations are preventing your friends from helping you. Only you can break down these barriers.

3: By becoming too isolated in self-pity or anger, you may have locked out friends and your higher self.

2: If you must help, do so without surrendering your self-worth and dignity. Volunteering for exploitation is a form of self-abuse.

1: There is a need to find a better balance in how you see your role and the degree of help you provide. Examine the boundaries you set for yourself.

Unchanging: Your frustration about this relationship will not abate until you adjust to the reality of its limitations. Do not try to force the issue or return things to a previous status. Accept what you cannot change and enjoy what good still remains.

42. Generosity

There are good opportunities to demonstrate your benevolence and reap the reward of your generosity. The fates will be exceptionally generous to you in providing openings to be recognized and admired for your good qualities and charitable behavior. Therefore, it is an excellent time for improving relations with others as well as with your higher self. Look to where possessiveness, small mindedness, pessimism, and fear of taking risks have prevented you from achieving what you want. By lifting your vision to a more abundant quality of thought and attitude, you can elevate all of your relationships and promote growth of character.

Dominant: The way to attract the favorable attention of important people is to demonstrate generosity in what you say and do. By restraining self-interest and serving the needs of others, you attract their cooperation and support.

Subordinate: Re-examine how you have defined the needs of others and your motives for helping them. Try to be more sensitive to their unique strengths and problems. Your benevolence and generosity of thought will be recognized and returned in kind.

THE CHANGING LINES

6: You may have assumed too much authority in this relationship. Adapt to the realities of the situation quickly or you may lose the respect of others.
5: Behavior stemming from a generous heart will reap great rewards even from the cynical and resentful.
4: You are in a position to counsel others to heal their differences. Be guided by the collective need and the healing potential in the situation.
3: The hidden benefit from a conflict with others will be revealed. Hold tight; patience and endurance are the keynotes.
2: Others become more receptive to you as they recognize that your intentions and goals are charitable and kind. Practice self-restraint.
1: You will accomplish little unless you act unselfishly. Discipline your desire to control or use people.

Unchanging: Be open to the clues and opportunities that can lead to a new understanding of your relationships and how to nurture them. Persistent generosity in thought and behavior will be required to meet these new opportunities.

43. Commitment

Inner forces of truth and wholeness are now at work to assist you in resolving old conflicts. However, to be completely successful, you may need to take a different approach to these differences. It is time to assert your authority over your own fears, doubts, resentments or other defensive habits. This will clear the way for more constructive thinking and behavior. Perhaps you have been hindered by your own obsession with conflict and the resulting irritation. Your attitude needs to be less reactive and more solution-oriented. Try to be more motivated by a love of good instead of guilt, anger, or despair. Seek to focus on the healthy potential you want to develop rather than your own frustrations. Reactivate your commitment.

Dominant: You may need to declare a new beginning in your relationship and begin working more to make the most of current opportunity and potential rather than fighting what is wrong or past events.

Subordinate: Be pragmatic rather than punitive. Look for the realistic potential in this situation and then be more forgiving and nurturing than firm and demanding, more encouraging than critical.

THE CHANGING LINES

6: Self-deception or over-confidence is blinding you to a fatal flaw in your judgment and plans. Rethink!
5: You must be thoroughly committed to succeed now. Elements of self-doubt, mixed motives, or ambivalent feelings stand in your way.
4: Little progress can be made because you may be too assertive or aggressive to recognize the needs and wants of others.
3: Retain your values, but realize that you may need to "go along to get along." There may be no other way to sustain this relationship.
2: Be on guard to deceit and manipulation by others. Clarify your psychological limits and boundaries.
1: Be sure your expectations are realistic and achievable. If they aren't, your efforts may backfire.

Unchanging: Your greatest obstacle to cultivating a healthy relationship lies within your own nature. It is time to review your values, expectations, motives, and attitudes. You may need a whole new understanding and approach plus dedicated effort to improve matters—a new level of commitment.

44. Jeopardy

This situation calls for you to clarify your values and hold fast to your ideals. Be very clear about what you expect and what you will not permit in yourself or in others. There is danger that you will be tempted to do something that will undermine your best interest in this relationship. It may be that you have the opportunity to take advantage of someone, or it may be that misguided love is causing you to indulge the bad habits of others. Or it may be that you have rationalized your use of blatant selfishness and manipulation to deal with others. In any case, beware doing what brings immediate comfort to yourself or others by appeasing the demands of the moment. Don't ignore the warning signals that tell you things are not as simple as they seem on the surface; subsequent events may eventually be explosive.

Dominant: Hidden problems may lurk beneath the surface of this relationship. If it seems too easy or too good to be true, it probably is. Be clear and forthright about your needs and values. Don't compromise your standards.

Subordinate: What seems proper at first may backfire. You may be tempted to take advantage of someone, especially since they may signal that this is what they want.

THE CHANGING LINES

6: Changes in this relationship may require you to withdraw somewhat. Do so quietly and graciously.
5: It is essential to let your principles and conscience guide you. You may be embarrassed unless you are firm with both yourself and others.
4: You may be overcautious and overly protective of your interests. Broaden your perspective.
3: This relationship has much to teach you about your confused motives and attitudes. Look for the message.
2: You know what to do, but you will need strong self-control to do it. Watch yourself!
1: Now is the time to control and neutralize a potential problem between yourself and others. Seize the opportunity before it passes.

Unchanging: There are signs that you are meeting your exact opposite in some ways. The result may be disastrous if you are naïve, stubborn, or defensive. Or it may be productive, if you use this opportunity to learn about yourself and human nature.

45. Partnership

By coordinating your efforts around a common theme, all parties will prosper. This is a time when your greatest success will come from contributing to the relationship, rather than trying to get something out of it. Therefore, set aside self-interest and view this relationship as a true partnership. Begin with a search for the higher purpose or themes that should guide all principals in this relationship. Study the situation to redefine your proper role in it. Look for the presence of values, attitudes, goals, problems, or work that you share. As you seek to serve these common interests, you will find what you need to do to reap the greatest success.

Dominant: Now is a time when you can gain the most by subordinating yourself to a noble purpose and/or serving the needs of powerful people. Decide what is appropriate and ethical for you to do and then go help them.

Subordinate: You will find correct guidance in the traditions that govern this kind of relationship. Out of your common background and shared needs, you will find the strength to enrich this relationship.

THE CHANGING LINES

6: Outer styles and objectives are in conflict. Harmony will be possible only if you make a major change in your motives, attitudes, and expectations.
5: To establish trust and rapport, you will need to earn it by demonstrating your wisdom and virtues.
4: Stress those goals that you share with others. This attracts their cooperation, and everyone can benefit.
3: Harmony will be difficult, but it may be possible if you seek to do the will of those in control.
2: Allow yourself to be more responsive to other people. Your natural reserve inhibits opportunities.
1: You are being too independent and too reluctant to share direction and authority with others. This opportunity may be lost for lack of commitment.

Unchanging: Your highest good is served by expanding your sense of identity to include the presence of another person or group. This will expand your view and attitude as well as guide you to a more fulfilling life.

46. Breakthrough

What you have long nurtured in a relationship now becomes possible. This is a natural outgrowth of your cultivation of social skills, correct motivation, the ability to be flexible, and your genuine affection for others. These continual efforts now make it possible for substantial progress to be made in important relationships, either to strengthen existing ones or build new relationships. People will be more receptive to you, and those in authority will listen to you. Success, however, will not come to you automatically. You will need to assert yourself and present plans or at least overtures for others to consider.

Dominant: You will find others quite receptive to you in those relationships where you have built up much trust and goodwill. Use this time to promote your legitimate interests. Persistent and steady efforts will be the effective way to do this.

Subordinate: Where you have been persistently affectionate and fair, you now find others are very responsive to you. Communications and cooperation are favored, but you must take the initiative.

THE CHANGING LINES

6: Others are not receiving what you think you are sending. Recheck your observations and assumptions and then revise your message.

5: The attitudes and habits that have led to your current success must be maintained or you will lose momentum.

4: If you don't change what works, you will become even more successful in the successful aspects of this relationship.

3: Don't let recent good results tempt you to take this success for granted. Keep up your discipline.

2: Your greatest asset in this relationship is your genuineness and trustworthiness. Demonstrate them.

1: You can attract favorable attention by showing others that you are a reliable worker and friend.

Unchanging: It will be necessary to make a long term investment in being productive, honest, and helpful in this relationship. You gain the trust and respect of others by these small, steady efforts.

47. Damage Control

This is a time when anything you say seems to be misunderstood or ignored. People are not receptive to your ideas or needs. Even your integrity and worth seem to be questioned. It will be very tempting to react with anger or anxiety, but this will only increase your frustration. The best course of action now is to keep faith in yourself and focus on preventing things from becoming even worse by your reaction to these events. Let steadfastness and caution be your key-words while you wait for better times to act and communicate. Concentrate on sustaining your sense of worth and positive expectation, and let your calm-ness and cheerful expectation speak for itself.

Dominant: Recheck your motives and plans, and then, if you are correct, do as little as possible. Spend your time preserving your strength and determination to act again when the time is right.

Subordinate: Since communications are not effective, speak by your actions. Demonstrate your thoughtful concern, integrity, and support in gesture and deed. Wait for better times to resolve conflicts.

THE CHANGING LINES

6: Your own pessimism has become part of your problem. You need to think more constructively.

5: There are important aspects of this situation you fail to understand. Frustrations and hurt egos are getting in the way. Keep calm until issues improve.

4: Do not permit frustration or defensiveness to make you compromise your principles. Success is delayed but will arrive if you are patient and restrained.

3: You have expected more than is possible and are now discouraged. You need to accurately reassess the potential in this relationship and act accordingly.

2: You need to revise your attitude. Perhaps some degree of your selfishness or neglect has harmed this relationship. Are you taking too much for granted?

1: Your own frustration is blinding you to the reality and potential of this relationship. Little will change until you change your attitude about it.

Unchanging: Your frustration may now seem complete because there is little you can say or do to change matters. Realize this fact and remain calm. Take no risks or impulsive action. Rely on your determination to survive.

48. Origins

The bonds we have with others are both superficial and deep. While matters of style and taste may seem important, shared values, purposes, and goals have far more power to build and sustain an enduring relationship. This is a time when it will be essential to concentrate on the inner aspects of the relationship. Study the nature of the forces or desires that drew you to this person—or group—in the first place. Search for a fresh understanding of their needs, wants, hopes, and dreams. This will enable you to know how to act toward others. If you merely concentrate on current conflicts or feelings, you will misunderstand what is unfolding at a deeper level. Success is favored if a more holistic view is taken and acted upon.

Dominant: You have been drawn to this relationship by something more profound than you suspect. Search for what is beneath your surface perceptions and feelings. Set aside your self-interest and reactions or you may miss the real opportunity that you have.

Subordinate: If you concentrate only on your wants and feelings, you will misunderstand the role that your higher self wants you to play. A deeper purpose has drawn you together. Let it unfold.

THE CHANGING LINES

6: You appear to be well attuned to others, and they warmly receive your ideas and suggestions.

5: Listen to your common sense, because you truly seem to know what to do. Concentrate on applications now.

4: Your best investment in a good relationship will be to get your own act together. Examine and revise your sense of purpose, role, and attitudes.

3: Be more creative and imaginative in this relationship. You have overlooked some possibilities to strengthen it.

2: You are underachieving because you are not making good use of your strengths. If you ignore them, so will others, and opportunities will be missed.

1: You have let inertia, old assumptions, and prejudice dull your mind. Until you have something better to offer, others will ignore you.

Unchanging: The situation is puzzling, and your own analysis and efforts may not be able to solve the problem. Seek the advice and help of others and your higher self. A collaborative effort involving you and your friends may lead to the best result.

49. Disappointment

There may be a serious misunderstanding by you or others about the nature and purpose of this relationship. It is now important to review even the most fundamental aspects of this relationship. Great disappointment or discord is possible, and it can be resolved only by careful, deliberate, and thoughtful changes. Study the situation. Open discussions and patience alone may resolve these differences. In other cases, the problem will be deeper and will require a careful restructuring of the relationship. To sustain it, you may need to redefine your role and your expectations as well as what you contribute to it. Make any changes slowly and cautiously. Keep flexible and alert to the response of others.

Dominant: Disappointment may occur because your concept of role, authority, and purpose in this relationship is different from the thinking of others. A new paradigm rather than just a new style may be needed. Be ready to compromise and adjust.

Subordinate: There are real or potential problems brewing. Simple moodiness may be the cause, or it may be something more basic. More discussion and observation are needed to decide what the issues are. A solution can come only out of great patience, clear understanding, and a great love for others.

6. For the moment, be content with the good elements of this relationship. Consolidate and build on your success rather than push for new changes.

5: Your good judgment and attitude are obvious, and you will find that others recognize this fact. Use this opportunity to initiate changes and reforms.

4: Be prepared for major changes. If you meet them with insight and fairness, success is likely.

3: Don't be easily intimidated into abandoning your position by changing times. If change becomes essential, then do so gradually and forthrightly.

2: Clear understanding and persistence will be required for the changes you will have to make.

1: Don't do anything if you are uncertain when to act or what to do. Wait until matters are clearer.

Unchanging: The relationship is unstable and something needs to be done to resolve the situation, yet the nature of these changes is unclear. Because you will need the support of others, check out their attitudes and opinions. This will help you define the potential in this relationship and refine your plans.

50. Readjustment

This is a time when you are more attuned to the order and design of subtle but powerful inner forces of your life. Consequently, new life is moving into you to inspire and promote a more enlightened bond with your higher self as well as others. As a result, all of your relationships may be affected. For some, this will mean adjusting to the reality of their fate or the consequences of their lack of responsibility. Others will find that new insights are showered on them or that there is new opportunity to express their creativity and plans. The key to success at this time is readjustment. If you reject selfishness and seek to think and act in harmony with the highest good of others, you will find your efforts are rewarded.

Dominant: Seek out a new view of others and their needs. If you listen to your intuition and conscience now, your choices and decisions are likely to be on target. Your greatest success will come through your efforts or sacrifices in response to the needs of others.

Subordinate: You can reduce conflict and establish greater harmony by a more charitable redefinition of your sense of limits, duties, and needs. Small efforts to cooperate or to sacrifice will bring great advances now.

6: Your common sense and conscience are now exceptionally clear, helping you understand your situation. Trust them and act decisively.

5: It may be time to adopt a more charitable and generous outlook toward others. Reject the expedient and honor your principles.

4: Your understanding is incomplete because you are overestimating the power or correctness of your position.

3: You may have become too passive or permissive. You need to assert your strengths and express your charm and virtues more effectively.

2: To improve your relationship, stop going with the flow and stand up for what you believe.

1: To achieve significant change in this relationship, you may need to consider new ways of handling it.

Unchanging: A new and more harmonious order and design is being promoted from your higher self as well as the higher realms of your group or family. Look for insights that can lead to a healthy readjustment in your lifestyle and toward others.

51. Shakeup

This is a time when something unexpected may occur in your relationships. These changes may not only surprise you but also destabilize your life for a while. This may well be something that you cannot avoid and must, therefore, accept. You can prepare for this shakeup by doing two things: first, identify with your basic strengths and principles so you can remain calm and in control, and second, stabilize your affairs as well as you can. These activities will help you to consolidate your resources so that you can cope with the unexpected with self-control and common sense. Depending on how well you conduct yourself, this situation can lead to substantial personal growth of self-awareness and virtue.

Dominant: The only thing you can control in this situation may be how you choose to react to it. Seek to be as calm and self-disciplined as possible. This is the only attitude which will allow you to respond with dignity and confidence.

Subordinate: This is a time to remain as calm and as sensible as possible. Focus on survival with your dignity intact. The surprising changes in this relationship will determine what you must do.

THE CHANGING LINES

6: Unexpected events may be so overwhelming that you need to withdraw and consult your innermost guidance rather than your confused feelings.

5: Don't be stubborn or outraged. It is vital to make a skillful adaptation to the changes in this relationship as it evolves and unfolds.

4: Stop letting your fears or confusion control you. Seek to be guided by your values, conscience, and principles.

3: A strategic retreat from this relationship may be in order, but don't panic. Keep calm and seek to reduce the threat.

2: It is necessary to withdraw from this relationship for the moment to avoid even greater harm or shock.

1: You are overreacting to an implied or perceived threat. You may need to do very little other than remain calm and wait out the situation.

Unchanging: Be prepared to accept the fact that you are not now and never have been the center of the universe. If you are ready to change your attitude and expectations—even your lifestyle—you can prevent much despair and anxiety.

52. A Peaceful Perspective

There is something inherently unpredictable about your relationship. Perhaps it is because someone is being indecisive, fickle, or just very emotional. As a result, it will be important to be as practical and as objective as possible. In particular, you must restrain your usual assumptions and avoid any projection of your beliefs or demands. Anticipate nothing, even if it means living one day—or even one hour—at a time. If you do this, you will be able to find inner peace and deal with people effectively and objectively. Sustaining this peaceful attitude will enable you to tap the power of your higher self to help guide you.

Dominant: Don't trust your usual instincts or reactions and don't try to use your customary approach to this relationship. Try to see it as wholly new, requiring new understanding and methods for success. Take your cues from what they do or don't do. Prepare to be innovative.

Subordinate: You may have allowed yourself to become stuck in prejudices or old assumptions that are blocking understanding and effective handling of this relationship. By contemplating the situation in a detached manner, you can rise above fears and doubts to recognize what needs to be done, if anything.

THE CHANGING LINES

6: To comprehend this relationship, you must reach a higher and more peaceful perspective. Deep contemplation will be essential to achieve this.

5: Your ego or your habit of assertiveness is misleading you. Cultivate detachment and inner peacefulness to establish a better relationship.

4: Pay attention to your common sense and do more to control your reactions and willfulness.

3. The order and tranquillity you seek cannot be imposed by an act of will; it requires your surrender to the inner peacefulness of your higher self.

2: There is an established momentum to your objectives and activities, and it will be essential to go mainly with this momentum rather than opposing it.

1: Continue to keep your perspective and motives set on discovery and investigation; this will provide the objectivity to manage this situation effectively.

Unchanging: This relationship is at a flexible and somewhat unstable state. No definitive pattern of its movement is emerging as yet. No advice can be given except to observe it carefully and respond to it as the relationship changes from moment to moment.

53. Moderation

The key to progress at this time lies in steady action in a traditional style. Confrontation, untraditional ideas, challenges, and other bold moves will be misunderstood or may cause offense. Therefore, this is a time when you need to work for a gradual and evolutionary development of this relationship. It means that you need to honor the good potential of this relationship and let it develop of its own accord. This calls for moderation, cooperation, patience, and integrity. Success can be fostered most effectively as you work within the context of the accepted social traditions that govern this relationship.

Dominant: It will be essential to practice patience and self-restraint. Any attempt at dazzling or aggressive moves may backfire. It is best to try to lead by demonstrating loyalty, competence, fairness, and trustworthiness. In this manner, small initiatives are accepted.

Subordinate: The relationship requires great tact and gentleness. Exercise caution and stick to a moderate pace and style of behavior. The shortest path to success now lies in slow but steady work to achieve your objectives.

THE CHANGING LINES

6. Your demonstration of patience, steadfastness, and loyalty will cause others to honor you.

5: Hold tight. Your authority and motives may be questioned or challenged, but the correctness of your position will be vindicated eventually.

4: Temporary conflicts may require that you plan a strategic retreat if you are to be successful later.

3: Beware the risk of bold moves. Forcing the issue now may jeopardize even what you have. Be patient.

2: You have established a reliable foundation for your relationship, and you can now build on this success.

1: You may need to refine your style and strategies. Listen to feedback and criticism and learn from them.

Unchanging: While you can map out many ways to manage this relationship, the process cannot be rushed. There is an innate design and pace that is governing its natural unfoldment and change. Do not try to be innovative or push this process; follow tradition.

54. Supportiveness

You have little control in this relationship. In fact, any effort to be assertive or to force an issue will be misunderstood. Rash statements will likely be used against you. If you are noticed, it will be only for the quality of support you give, rather than who you are. If you stand out in any way, you may attract criticism or envy. Therefore, it is essential that you play a carefully limited and supportive role. Your well-being is dependent on staying in the good graces of others. Understand the kinds of communication and behavior that are expected of you and perform them well. Hold fast to your principles, and plan for better times after this phase of dependency passes.

Dominant: You are being strictly limited by the expectations and even whims of others. For the moment, let them set the agenda, standards, and the pace. Success comes in meeting their standards of loyalty and competence.

Subordinate: Learn to become a good follower and aim solely to please, since that is all you are permitted to do at the moment. Exercise special care in finding out exactly what others want; any confusion in communications will be disastrous at this time.

THE CHANGING LINES

6: You need to be more sincere in your efforts to serve or satisfy others. Put your heart into it.

5: Overcome your reluctance to doing what others want. Your success will depend on identifying and serving the needs of others.

4: It is essential for now to reduce your efforts to simply surviving. Preserve your integrity and save your energies for better times.

3: You will need to use great flexibility to adapt to the demands of challenging people and situations. Are you sure this is worthwhile?

2: This relationship takes much more than it gives. Your well-being depends on your own determination and loyalty to the original ideal of the relationship.

1: You are limited to the role of being a helper or advisor to those who actually wield authority.

Unchanging: Any real progress in this relationship will depend on a thorough clarification of the nature of your role and what you expect for yourself and from others. Until this is changed, you will experience only more of the same.

55. Prospering Times

This is a time of high tide in personal relationships. People will pay attention to what you say, give you recognition for your contributions, praise your talent, and cooperate with your wishes. Your natural charm and creativity are at a peak level, and you can expect this to increase your success in many ways. In established relationships, you can concentrate on enhancing the quality of it and in deepening bonds of trust and affection. In new or limited relationships, you may be able to extend it to include friendship. But remember that the high tide is followed by an ebbing of energy and success. Therefore, while it lasts, use this moment to your advantage.

Dominant: This is a brief time when you will be exceptionally lucky and prosperous in your relationships. Be careful that your confidence and exuberance do not exceed your abilities and energies or you may find you have overcommitted yourself.

Subordinate: You are now able to attract the favorable attention of others and will be exceptionally lucky in relationships. But beware the temptation to abandon your principles for this period of luck will not last.

THE CHANGING LINES

6: This relationship may be too dominated by your attempts to control or possess. Permit more freedom.

5: Your view of this relationship is clouded by your emotions. Seek the advice and counsel of others to regain a realistic perspective.

4: The situation is becoming more favorable for you; therefore, hold to your plans and expectations.

3: If you manage this situation with tolerance and patient understanding, the relationship survives and improves.

2: Your position is weak and influence minimal. You can increase your rapport only with a demonstration of patience and gentleness.

1: You need a mentor or experienced advisor to help you manage the rough spots of this relationship.

Unchanging: Unusual good luck for you now dominates this relationship. But be careful that you do not lose your perspective about yourself or others. An excess of any good thing can lead to mischief and harm unless you act with caution and great discernment.

56. Uncharted Seas

You are entering new and unexplored psychological territories. Perhaps this relationship is new or you are entering a new or rapidly changing aspect of it. In any case, the status of this relationship will not remain as it is, so proceed with caution and without definite expectations or commitments. Because there is much that you have yet to comprehend about this relationship as well as your own desires and goals, you need to act prudently. Use this time to explore and learn about others as well as yourself. Curb your judgments as well as your feelings or attempts to control until there is greater clarity about where you stand and where you are headed.

Dominant: Give this relationship a light touch, because it or you or both are in the process of change. Only short range, modest goals are possible. Keep your options open.

Subordinate: Much about this relationship is unknown or undefined; therefore, you must now play a modest role and be very clear about your boundaries, limits, and sense of where you stand.

THE CHANGING LINES

6: You are in danger of losing your clear sense of identity and focus. Step back and examine your purpose in this relationship.

5: You need to reposition yourself in this relationship. Clarify your boundaries and limits and review your basic beliefs.

4: If this relationship is to grow, you will have to set aside your doubts and accept some basic change in it and yourself.

3: Beware! You may be trying to control someone who can be handled only with tact and diplomacy.

2: A show of confidence and cheerfulness will now elicit the attention and support of the very people you wish to attract.

1: Stop acting helpless and feeling sorry for yourself. Be proud of who you are and others will respect you for it.

Unchanging: The relationship has become stagnant or never gone beyond a superficial phase, because you have allowed yourself to become complacent and unimaginative. It is time to find new options and opportunities.

57. Respect

Some achievements require mutual trust and steady work toward a common goal. Genuine relationships are built of the same qualities and shared endeavors. Coercion, intimidation, and exploitation are fatal in these relationships, as they would be now in the subject of your inquiry. To be a constructive influence in this relationship, you must elicit amicable cooperation. Therefore, proceed with the utmost patience and gentleness, respecting the needs and limitations of the others involved. Only a long lasting effort will produce worthwhile results. Short cuts and bold moves will fail. Take time to refine your understanding of the potential to be developed in this relationship. Be led by what potential you find rather than your own desires and whims.

Dominant: Avoid independent decision and action. If your relationship is to a group, be led by the example of its dominant leader. If you are relating to an individual, be led by his or her needs and higher self.

Subordinate: The relationship calls for an unselfish contribution on your part. Avoid your usual assumptions. Study this person or group to determine what you can do to help them progress in their growth and development and then do it.

THE CHANGING LINES

6: Your progress has been limited because you have spent too much time in analysis and planning.
5: The health of this relationship is dependent on sustaining your constructive efforts. Be steadfast.
4: By persistent modest efforts, you can overcome the resistance to what you are convinced must change.
3: You are indulging in too much speculation and are in danger of losing the respect and attention of others. Be more practical and constructive.
2: Look for undercurrents of ambivalence, resistance, and doubt that are sabotaging this relationship.
1: Your lack of clarity and decision is preventing progress in this relationship.

Unchanging: What this relationship requires is mutual respect and assistance. Do not attempt to project your usual assumptions and beliefs on others. Instead, take time to discover and respect their innate needs. Only by doing this can you decide what, if anything, you can do to enhance this relationship.

58. Friendship

Openness and friendliness in all relationships will create a climate of cheerfulness and optimism. This will be a time for effective communication and building closer bonds of trust and affection. People will respond favorably to your friendly words and gestures. Any encouragement given will be received as a sign of your sincerity and goodwill. Others will also tend to be trusting and encouraging to your efforts. But beware of an excess of trust and generosity. Gullibility may also be a problem as you or others make too much of superficial gestures and charisma or become lost in the joy of the moment. Some may be tempted to exploit others' trust and kindness at this time.

Dominant: Old barriers to trust and communication will be weakened. Others will be more open to discussions about difficult or forbidden topics. This is a great time to foster cooperation and loyalty by supporting the goals and well-being of others.

Subordinate: The shell of independence and "toughness" in others will be less during this period. Use this time to foster better communications and trust by demonstrating your loyalty and affection.

THE CHANGING LINES

6: You are risking becoming too involved in the wants of others at the expense of your own needs.
5: Be careful of relationships that exploit your goodwill and helpfulness. Review your values and needs.
4: It is important to take a long range view of relationships or you may miss the greater value in people who are less dazzling but more mature.
3: You are in danger of being misled by momentary optimism and superficial friendliness.
2: You can find your way out of your confused emotions and wasted efforts by focusing more attention on your principles and values.
1: The respect that you seek from others can often be found in yourself as you renew your faith in your own worth and your commitment to your values.

Unchanging: This is not a time for fierce independence. Your success now requires that you focus on what you can share with others. Sincere respect and thoughtfulness about the welfare of others will bring big dividends.

59. Fellowship

That which is broken needs to be mended. Those who are alienated need to be drawn back into the fellowship of others. Relationships which are strained need to be healed. This is a time when you should strive for a reunion with others and within yourself. For some, there is a need to examine their mixed feelings and motives about others and themselves. The focus for this reunion may be physical, emotional, or spiritual. Seek out the values, sense of purpose, or heritage that you share with others. Strive to discover and reunite with these elements that can help you rise above mundane events and memories. This can be the basis for reunion with others as well as the disparate parts of yourself.

Dominant: Avoid any one-sided effort to assert your independence or special "rights" now. This is a time when your interests are best served by supporting the collective purpose and mutual benefits that arise out of a healthy relationship.

Subordinate: An investment of optimism, tolerance, and forgiveness may pay big dividends at this time. Focus your attention on the fact of previous benefits and the current good potential of this relationship. This effort will help you transcend and heal real or potential differences.

THE CHANGING LINES

6: It is important to take steps to reduce conflict and tensions, even if it means a temporary separation.

5: The basis for improving this relationship lies in focusing on the real and hidden benefits of sharing and cooperation.

4: You need a new vision of the good potential in this relationship to lead you out of petty divisions.

3: This relationship will be successful only if you give top priority to promoting it.

2: Your own fear, guilt, or resentment is the main obstacle to cultivating a better relationship.

1: Do not overlook the smallest misunderstanding or disagreement, as you can still prevent small conflicts from becoming major conflicts.

Unchanging: There is an odd estrangement in this relationship. You may be too stuck on just one narrow perspective or attitude. Perhaps the problem lies in your wounded ego or your misunderstanding of events. Improvement may depend on you seeking a new and more holistic view of this relationship.

60. Self-Control

Without restraint we become unfocused and our path ahead is poorly defined. We need to be guided by a sense of identity and the purpose we serve. Our behavior needs to be restrained and defined by our principles, the role that we are to play, and objectives we strive to reach. Likewise, in relationships, we need to strive for sensible restraint in what we expect of others in terms of their loyalty, friendship, and contribution. If we expect too much or are too strict, we provoke resistance and conflict. If we are too permissive, others do not know where they stand with us or assume that we are indifferent. Review the nature of your role and the quality of your standards and expectations in this relationship.

Dominant: Your authority is more limited in this relationship than you suspect. To prevent misunderstanding and rebellion, you need to make realistic and fair adjustments in what you demand of others. By streamlining your attitudes you earn their affection and loyalty.

Subordinate: Your attitude may be too idealistic or resentful, for it is not in harmony with reality in this relationship. Respect the limitations of others and restrain your efforts to convert or reform them. This will reduce tension and conflict.

6: You need to be more self-controlled than controlling of others. You are demanding too much.

5: Ask of others only what you are willing to accept for yourself. This will demonstrate your fairness.

4: Set aside your ideals and lofty theories in favor of adjusting yourself to the reality of the situation.

3: Much of the strain in this relationship is due to your excesses and impulsiveness. Accept your responsibility and work on correcting your mistakes.

2: Do not wait too long to work at improving this relationship or the opportunity may be lost.

1: Recognize and accept the real limitations in this relationship rather than attempting to overcome them. This will preserve your strength and integrity.

Unchanging: The key to this relationship is pragmatism. Your thinking and emotions are confused and nebulous. You need to clarify the potential of this relationship as well as your role in it. Once you have defined these, you will know what to do.

61. The Mystery

There are times when our lack of vision and understanding permit shallow assumptions and prejudice to rule us. This misunderstanding can cause us to view the character and behavior of others in a distorted manner, as though they were a mystery to us. Consequently, we are unable to make effective judgments or decisions. Disharmony is the inevitable consequence. Only adequate knowledge can correct this problem, and this knowledge can come only by a sincere effort to comprehend the innermost thoughts and attitudes of others. We need to speculate about what this relationship seems like from the other person's perspective. Only then can we adequately understand and relate to them.

Dominant: Your relationship may lack depth and richness because you are too focused on the superficial details of it. To enrich the rapport and cooperation in this relationship, you need to try to see life from their viewpoint. For a start, try to be more open to them.

Subordinate: Most people are not telepathic nor do they bother with people who try to remain mysterious. You may need to be more expressive and less subtle and manipulative in making your needs and wants known.

THE CHANGING LINES

6: You may know what you want in this relationship but others are not ready to provide this. Be sensible!
5: You are respected as a person of authority and will be given respect and loyalty. Accept these.
4: Even if others cannot follow it, you need more idealism about your role in this relationship.
3: You may have become too attentive to the approval of others to judge your worth and appropriateness.
2: You have an unusually close and effective rapport with others; they will listen to you now.
1: Base your decisions and behavior on your common sense, experience, and principles. The advice or example of others can mislead you.

Unchanging: Despite what you assume, you are as much a mystery to others as they are to you. The relationship in question cannot progress until you reveal more of yourself and enrich your understanding of their attitude, intentions, and expectations.

62. The Razor's Edge

There are times when we seem to walk a figurative razor's edge between extremes of potential disaster. This is one such period in your life. It will be essential to be as pragmatic as possible. Attend to the smallest details in this relationship. Do not fail to miss hints and suggestions that will provide important clues as to what you need to do or stop doing. Avoid any dramatic show of your talent or strengths lest you provoke competition or opposition. Humility will serve you far better than assertiveness. Strive for modest goals and adhere to a conservative, polite, and traditional style in this relationship. This course of action will prevent many problems.

Dominant: Your authority and influence may be less than it seems. Others may have changed or they are being more fickle—or simply more insecure. It is important to be cautious and practical. Assume little and risk less until you reassess the situation.

Subordinate: Overcome your resistance to playing a modest and cooperative role for the moment. Overt displays of emotion or manipulation may backfire right now. Invest your energies in doing your duty and in earning the respect and loyalty of others.

THE CHANGING LINES

6: Your expectations may be unrealistic and your efforts too aggressive. Restrain yourself now before your lose everything.
5: Either you misunderstand others or are misunderstood by them, and this prevents your success. Others can help you fill in the gaps of your knowledge.
4: Seek a more modest role and goal in this relationship now. Aggressive moves will fail.
3: Do not become complacent and take the goodwill and loyalty of others for granted. Look for hints of potential conflict or misunderstanding.
2: You need to make this relationship more secure and stable by cultivating the loyalty and support of others.
1: Only modest goals and plans will be effective now. Anything greater may place tremendous strain on the relationship.

Unchanging: It will be vital to conduct yourself in a responsible way and to perform your duties as tradition would define them. Simplify your demands and don't make waves, for the best you can do is to maintain your position.

63. Vulnerability

The tides of human affairs can take us to peaks of success and happiness. We can reach a degree of contentment and fulfillment in relationships. Unfortunately, it is an illusion that this success will last forever. Situations change just as we and others change. This relationship now may seem to be at a phase of relative stability or harmony, but it may not endure. Your best course of action is to enjoy any success, but be attentive to small hints or signs that disharmony is brewing. Be vigilant about recognizing potential sources of friction before they erupt. Put more effort into maintaining the relationship. Take little for granted; assume little. Be frank and open and frequent in your discussions.

Dominant: Do not be lulled by current success or harmony in this relationship. Your position is vulnerable. Be attentive to hints of disharmony or resistance and work now to minimize their effect.

Subordinate: Old bonds of loyalty and respect are shifting and being redefined. You can avoid much frustration by recognizing this and learning to accommodate these changes while actively participating in the evolution of this relationship.

THE CHANGING LINES

6: You must remain vigilant and attentive to your responsibilities in this relationship or you may risk the loss of your investment in it.
5: Stick to a modest and simple style of behavior to achieve harmony and success in this relationship.
4: Beware! There is a strong potential for friction in this relationship.
3: Only persistent and skillful effort will enable you to cultivate and enrich this relationship. You may need to consult experts for advice.
2: You can redeem yourself and save your reputation by total honesty and acceptance of responsibility.
1: It is too late to revise your plans and goals about this relationship without obvious consequences. If it is worth it, go ahead anyway.

Unchanging: Your authority in this situation is weak and there is little that you can do to influence this relationship at the moment. Your best course is to accept the changes and play the role of a detached observer, thereby reducing your own distress.

64. Conclusions

All events eventually lead to a conclusion. Trends finally develop to a peak level and then reverse themselves. So also, many aspects of a relationship will reach a peak level and then move on to a different phase. Perhaps only some aspect of the relationship will end, or perhaps our role in it will change, but some change is inevitable. This relationship is now passing through a phase where much of it seems very familiar and routine. Your experience and mastery of your role provides you with an easy understanding of others and enables you to favorably influence or lead them. While there is much good potential in this relationship, it may soon change in a way that leads you into unfamiliar areas. Be cautious and reserved.

Dominant: Do not become complacent with the current status. You may soon find yourself in a very revised role in this relationship. New goals and strategies may be required. Seek counsel from your higher self.

Subordinate: You may have become too accustomed to something comfortable and reliable in this relationship. You may soon find the need to be more self-reliant in some way. Be prepared for a significant change in this relationship.

THE CHANGING LINES

6: Enjoy what success you have, but preserve some energy and imagination for the next phase of this relationship.

5: You are near a peak level of competence and effectiveness in this bond. Use your influence wisely.

4: You will need to rally all your strength and persistence to deal with the conflict at hand.

3: Realize that there are major limits in the potential of this relationship. To avoid frustration, lower your expectations or try something else.

2: What you seek to develop in this relationship is proper, but you need to wait for a better opportunity to achieve it.

1: Do little until the issues and complications of the current relationship are more clear and stable.

Unchanging: You may be hesitating too long about making a decision which will strongly alter your position in this relationship. Do not let fear of change or the unfamiliar put you in a limbo of inactivity. Be realistic and review your options as well as the consequences of trying to do nothing.

I CHING ON LINE

This book, *Connecting Lines,* is the complete text of the relationships module for *I Ching On Line,* a computer program adapting the I Ching to personal computers. *I Ching On Line* is available in versions both for the Macintosh and IBM PC (and compatibles).

The complete package includes the program plus four modules. The four modules being developed are: the healing module, the decision making module, the relationships module, and the personal growth module. The program plus all four modules can be ordered as a package for $100.

To order the complete I Ching On Line, send a check or money order to Ariel Press, 14230 Phillips Circle, Alpharetta, GA 30201 or call toll free, 1-800-336-7769, Monday through Thursday, 8 a.m. to 6 p.m., and charge the order to VISA, MasterCard, or American Express. In Georgia, please add 6 percent sales tax.

Connecting Lines, Ruling Lines, and *Healing Lines,* can also be bought and used independently of the computer program. The fourth book in the series will be called *Changing Lines.* These books may be bought for $7.95 apiece (plus $1.50 for shipping), or $30 for the set of four, postpaid.

In ordering the computer program, please specify the size of floppy disk used by your system.